SUITED FOR SUCCESS

25 INSPIRATIONAL STORIES ON GETTING PREPARED FOR YOUR JOURNEY TO SUCCESS

SUITED FOR SUCCESS

25 INSPIRATIONAL STORIES ON GETTING PREPARED FOR YOUR JOURNEY TO SUCCESS

PK KERSEY

SUITED FOR SUCCESS
Published by Purposely Created Publishing Group™

Copyright © 2018 PK Kersey

All rights reserved.

No part of this book may be reproduced, distributed or transmitted in any form by any means, graphic, electronic, or mechanical, including photocopy, recording, taping, or by any information storage or retrieval system, without permission in writing from the publisher, except in the case of reprints in the context of reviews, quotes, or references.

Printed in the United States of America

ISBN: 978-1-947054-97-4

Special discounts are available on bulk quantity purchases by book clubs, associations and special interest groups.
For details email: sales@publishyourgift.com
or call (888) 949-6228.

For information logon to:
www.PublishYourGift.com

Table of Contents

Foreword ix

Chapter 1: Black Men Rock
PK Kersey 1

Chapter 2: You Don't Know My Story
Shannon Lanier 11

Chapter 3: #EVERYBODYMatters
Charles A. Archer 25

Chapter 4: Faith. Grind. Inspire.
Dr. Jean Alerte 35

Chapter 5: Full Circle
Jamael Thompson 45

Chapter 6: Achieve Your Version of Success
Aaron S. Jenkins 55

Chapter 7: Let Your Situation Be Your Motivation
Randall E. Toby 65

Chapter 8: I Am Not a Bastard
Dr. Oliver T. Reid 77

Chapter 9: You're Not Good Enough
George Rice III 89

Chapter 10: You're a Winner
Larry Scott Blackmon..................................... 103

Chapter 11: Life Is Good!
Dwayne Booker... 117

Chapter 12: Statistics
Derrick J. Redmond 125

Chapter 13: Catalytic Leadership
Paul Coty 139

Chapter 14: Rising Above Feelings of Rejection
Steven Carter... 151

Chapter 15: Secrets to Employment Success
Craig Palma 165

Chapter 16: The "Facts" of My Life
Xavier Porter... 175

Chapter 17: The Path to Success
Troy Harrison 179

Chapter 18: RISE! From Thought to Fruition
David Marquis... 191

Chapter 19: Till Faith No Longer Possesses Parameters
Norman Grayson 199

Chapter 20: Trend God
Sherrod Kersey 211

Chapter 21: Mentoring
Darrell J. Edmonds.. 223

Chapter 22: The Latter Shall Be Greater
Dimitri David Jr. 229

Chapter 23: What Came First, the Growth or the Pain?
Cyriac St. Vil... 239

Chapter 24: Metamorphosis: Transforming Yourself into What You Need to Become
Conrad W. Higgins.. 253

Chapter 25: My Death Gave Birth to a New Me
Ty Brown 265

Sources... 273

About the Authors 275

Foreword

To me, Pastor Gerard Kersey is a remarkable individual. As his pastor, I have watched and discerned the call of God on his life. He is not just someone with a strong spiritual pulse but a family man, a family man who loves his wife and his children dearly. He has proven himself to be a leader, not only in his church but in his home. The scriptures teach us that "we will know them – not by their words, but by their fruits" (Matthew 7:15). Pastor Gerard Kersey has taken the time to write a book that I believe will bless those who understand that leadership is not a right but a privilege, and that leading is never easy but requires Godly wisdom.

I believe that every "life" will face challenges and hardships, however, we can be encouraged to know that if others have risen above their circumstances, we can too. In the mind of God, there is no defeat, no trouble, and no pain. But we as spirit beings, trapped in this human body, will face adversity for the purposes of mastering the human experience.

Many books are written, but not many inspire. I believe that this book is a *must-read* for anyone who has faced adversity but who still always believed that there's light at the end of the tunnel.

This book is designed to be evidence that our trials were never meant to derail us, but rather to propel us into our destiny. It is my prayer that, as you turn the pages of this book, your mind will be renewed, your heart encouraged, and your life forever changed. "For as a man thinketh, in his heart so is he" (Proverbs 23:7).

Paul B. Mitchell
Sr. Pastor, Changing Lives Christian Center

Chapter 1

Black Men Rock

PK Kersey

I know... I know... that is not an original title for my chapter. Black women have been rocking the world for over 10 years now. In my opinion, they've been rocking since the beginning of time, but that's another story. I love how black women celebrate one another and cheer each other on. I am a big social media user, and throughout my timeline, I see a women's conference here, an empowerment seminar here, etc. Women are really capitalizing on the power of unity and collaboration. The truth is, I love it and pray they continue because that is where true power lies.

Speaking of social media, one day as I was going through Facebook, I saw a post by the talented brand strategist, Shadé Adu. She was seeking individuals to be a part of her book project

Renegotiating Greatness: 21 Lessons from Bold Entrepreneurs Who Have Built Successful Brands. Having worked with her before, I knew this was something I wanted to jump on. I immediately contacted her and confirmed my spot. To my surprise, I was the only male on the project. It was then that I realized that I could not let women monopolize this collaboration key. I started planning ways to bring men together so that we can see the measure of success women are seeing. Men, especially black men, have long had the stigma that: we will not stick together nor support one another; we will not share information, networks, or success secrets; and that we are not hard-working, but shallow, insensitive, and lazy. People have many stereotypes and images of us that are not accurate at all. I know they are not accurate because I personally know plenty of black men that are just the opposite. I was fortunate to be included in the *Black Enterprise* series, *Modern Men*, where they celebrated black men who are changing the narrative. It is an awesome collection of amazing men who are taking their fate into their own hands and helping the next generation to achieve even more. Some of those modern men are included in this book. I believe the stories here will be lessons that we will look to for years to come. I put this book together to show the world that no matter where you start, no matter what challenges you face, no matter how hard it seems—SUCCESS IS POSSIBLE. The stories you read here are empowering, transparent, honest, powerful, and life changing. Some of these men I know personally and some I don't, but what I do know is that they have put in work. After reading this book, you will no longer be able to say, "I can't" because of reading the stories of so many who did! And one day (yes, I said it), we will turn on BET, Centric, or OWN and see black men rock!!!

Growing up in Brooklyn, New York, in the 70s was not an easy task. It was tough and challenging. Brooklyn 2017 is a whole lot different from Brooklyn 1970. Not that today is Heaven, but it is a gentler and kinder version of itself. That is a good thing. I am the oldest of three children that lived with my mother and stepfather (I have another brother from my biological father), so I had no big brother to assist me with schools, bullies, and such. I had to hold it down on my own. Also, I was not a tough kid; I was more of an introvert and a huge computer geek. I mean, I played sports heavy, but I wasn't a fighter. That being the case,

I had to have a lot of male friends to feel safe in the streets of Brooklyn. It was there that I learned a lot of my ways. With both parents working, I spent a lot of my days hanging with my friends. Among boys in that era, you could not show any weakness, you did not help each other, you did not celebrate each other, nor did you hide each other's shortcomings. In fact, we made fun of as many shortcomings as we could. We ridiculed any sign of weakness. It was unrelenting. At no moment could you lapse from being on your game because it would be exposed immediately and aggressively. It was during those years, and from my friends, that I received my training on being a man. We knew no other way. This was what we learned from the older kids and would teach the younger ones. I believe many men have the same example from their childhood memories. As a result of being boys who did not help each other, boys who did not celebrate one other, and boys who did not hide friends' shortcomings, we become men who have these same characteristics. I was fortunate to have both parents in my household. That gave me some balance and aided in my ability to mature my mindset. I gradually moved out of that mindset as my younger brother came along, I attended college, and the teachings of my parents began to take hold. However, many of those boys did not have both parents or alternative teaching to assist them, so they kept that mindset. Often, when I am in a workplace or at an event, I will speak to men and get no reply. Or they may say, "Hello" with their mouth but, "Get away from me" with everything else. While there could be many reasons for this, I often think that their childhood or how they were raised plays a role. Men who were isolated will not collaborate or build with other men. They might even be extremely successful, but only as an individual, not as a part of a community. I believe many good things can be done alone, but great and amazing things can only be done together.

Wake Up Call

Often during this life journey, we have encounters with people or go through circumstances that seem insignificant to the big picture. Things happen to us and we believe that they have no bearing on our life, but I must disagree with that. I believe that every circumstance we encounter and every person we come across plays a role in our development and the process of our success. Whenever I meet someone, I try to get their name, profession, and strike up a quick conversation because I have seen my life change drastically because of relationships.

I encourage you to speak to more people, step out of your comfort zone, smile, and talk about your true vision and dreams. Follow the example of every person in this book and change your life by doing what you thought you couldn't do.

After finishing high school and dabbling in college (I say dabbling because I didn't graduate), it was fortunate that I took a test with the state of New York and got a job with the motor vehicles department. Let me backtrack. I was a great high school student, but a horrible college student. I really cannot say I tried. I was so interested in coming out of my introverted shell that I fell in love with dancing (it was the hip hop, house era), and lost my mind with house music. I figured that I would work at the motor vehicles department for a little while until I got a better job. I stayed there for 24 years. I got promoted to the position of office manager and learned valuable information throughout my years. I was pretty much on cruise control with my life until one day we got an email from the governor stating that we would be receiving a one percent raise that year. We had not received a raise in two years. I realized that my salary, vacation, days off, and lunches were determined by other people. I was basically working at a place I didn't want to be, for a salary I didn't want, and a supervisor I couldn't stand. I had to grasp that my choices led me there and my choices could lead me out.

I had always wanted to do something big as far as being a business owner, I just didn't know what. I tried WorldVentures, Prepaid Legal, Primerica, Ambit, etc., but nothing clicked. One day I said, "Lord, how can I make more money?" The answer I heard was, "Give away suits to men in need." "What?" I asked. "How can giving away suits to men impact my bottom line? I mean, it's great for them but what about me?" Little did I know, that moment would change my entire life. It wasn't so much the giving away of suits as it was the obedience to what He said. While I was working a giving principal (give and it shall be given back to you), I was also walking into my purpose. Unbeknownst to me, all those years at the motor vehicles department, all the failed businesses, and all the arguments with DMV management was a part of this process. I liken it to the movie *The Karate Kid* where all he thought he was doing was washing the master's car and painting the master's house when he was actually preparing himself for his future greatness. We never enjoy or look forward to the process, but it makes or breaks us. I truly believe that everyone can achieve an incredible level of greatness, but it requires completing that process.

Time to Level Up

I can no longer tolerate people saying that they don't have time to focus on their vision or dreams. To me, that is no longer acceptable. When someone tells me that, all I hear is that they don't want to, they are too lazy, or they are happy where they are. I would prefer that they say those things instead of saying that they don't have time. When I received the message to give away suits to men, I had no clue where I should start. During the process of giving the vision life, I was married, a father of two, working a job at NYS DMV (you know how crazy that place is), an assistant pastor at my church, and taking care of a sick uncle. In no way did I have time to start a nonprofit, run a social media management company, and author four books. However, as I began to listen to motivational videos daily for encouragement, I realized I had to do it. There is no way you can listen to Les Brown, Myles Munroe, Tony Robbins, and Mel Robbins among others, and not be pushed to action. I realized I had to make the time to achieve my greatness. I had to learn my passion, enhance my gifts, and increase my knowledge. I truly saw no way out of my DMV job until I began to feed my spirit and mind with positivity and believe that wealth was possible for me and my family. There is something

Suited for Success

about belief that changes your outlook. There is a big difference between believing that you are a failure who is trying to be successful and believing that you are successful and resisting failure. So, I pushed myself to get up earlier, and work during my lunch break and after work. I make time to exercise, meditate, and plan my days.

No one said success would be easy, but it is definitely possible and well worth it. Success is truly working hard, with no apparent results for years, knowing the ultimate results will soon appear. Success is also a continual thing. Once you reach one level, you get more ideas and have a desire to reach new levels. As you do, you teach others who want to come with you, just as I was a part of Shadé's book and took others to make my own. Someone in this book will do the same because success begets success. As for the suits God told me to give away, not only was That Suits You started over five years ago, but it has suited over 7,300 individuals, trained thousands of individuals, and inspired millions. We have been fortunate to have been supported by HBO, ABC, NBC, and MLB among many others. Something that was only a thought had the ability to change the trajectory of my life. But, I had to give birth to what was in my heart! I implore you to not let the dream lie dormant. I beg you to not allow fear to reign supreme. Life is too short to work for years at a place you hate when greatness is only a heartbeat away!

Chapter 2

You Don't Know My Story

Shannon Lanier

The story of my life may look pretty perfect, at least on social media. You see me as an Emmy Award-winning television show host and global news anchor that has a smart and beautiful wife, three charming kids, and a huge home, but my story didn't start where I am now. These days, you may know me from my work as a TV host on *Arise Entertainment 360*, a correspondent on *Our World with Black Enterprise* or anchor on *FiOS1 News* in New York. Many have seen me interview tons of celebrities like Alicia Keys, Ne-Yo, Patti LaBelle, Tyler Perry, Mary J. Blige, Terrence Howard, and Taraji P. Henson to name a few.

If you don't watch much TV, you may also be familiar with my famous relative, President Thomas Jefferson. I am the great, great-great-

great-great-great-grandson of Jefferson and his slave, Sally Hemings, through their son, Madison Hemings. Several years ago, I was blessed enough to publish a book (with Random House) about my family called, *Jefferson's Children: The Story of One American Family*. I co-authored the book with photojournalist, Jane Feldman. The book takes readers on a journey to meet other descendants of Jefferson, both through his wife Martha's side of the family as well as his slave Sally's side of the family. We spoke to four generations of descendants of all ages.

I always tell people you may be surprised about what you find in your family if you start to do a little research. In my family, I've found doctors, lawyers, teachers, politicians, and now a TV personality. But on the other hand, I've also found some weed heads, racists, jail birds, and people who never did anything with their lives. Hey, you can't pick your family, right? We've all got some "characters" don't we? I know I'm not the only one with a drunk uncle who comes around to hit on all his cousins. Nasty! Right! You should see him chasing the young girls around, with his walker mind you, like, "Come over here, Girl. Don't make me break a hip."

Coming from a "famous family," people don't expect me to mention all the skeletons, but I keep it real. Like the fact that I recently found out that I have four uncles and an aunt that I never knew existed. They are my grandfather's other kids that neither I nor my father ever met because my grandfather left town when my dad was three years old. The point I'm trying to make is that while you may see someone like me and say, "Check him out. He's on TV with celebrities and living in New York City, he's got money, so he must have it so easy. He came from a rich family and sailed right on through life. His life and family must be perfect." Well, let me set the record straight... "You Don't Know My Story."

There is a popular gospel song by Vashawn Mitchell that says,

> "You don't know my story, all the things that I've been through;
>
> you can't feel my pain, what I had to go through to get here."

I love those lyrics because they are so true and hit home daily. You never know what someone had to go through for you to see them sit where they are today. I think that's why one of my favorite questions to ask celebrities is, "What was your first job before you were famous?" We see the fame and fortune now, but we don't know their story. We don't know that they were homeless or worked at McDonald's for cash. How they may have been a bad kid but turned their life around. Everyone has a story.

Take me for example. People may see where I am now (and let me mention, I'm still very far from where I want to end up) and not realize that growing up I wasn't rich, and we didn't have it easy. My dad had to work two and three jobs sometimes just to make ends meet. There was a period when times really got hard. I remember my mom making sure my brother, Shawn, and I were extra clean before we went to bed so the mice wouldn't bite us while we were sleeping. No, she wasn't just saying we couldn't eat late night snacks because we didn't really have any more food (although that was the case in some situations). Mom was looking out for our safety. Sometimes my dad would bring a few extra meals home from one of the restaurants he worked at just so we could eat. Then, there was the time we got evicted from one of our homes and had to move in with my dad's friend, and this dude had roaches. Not just a few that scattered when you turned on the lights. He had a lot of those down-home, big, fat, nasty, hood roaches. I remember turning on the lights once and a roach turned to me ready to box and was like, "Yo, I know you better turn that light back out! Don't start none won't be none." Ok, maybe it didn't happen exactly like that, but as a kid, that's how I interpreted it!

Don't get me wrong, we weren't dirt poor my whole childhood, but long enough. My parents worked very hard to get us out of those situations, and I'm so blessed because they worked hard to love us through them too. Most of the time, we didn't even know we were poor. Shoot, we have a lot of good memories thanks to my parents' determination to give us the best life possible, despite our economic situation. I remember always going to Holiday Inn to swim and eat, not realizing we were sneaking into one of the places where my father worked. The swimming pool was our babysitter and we had the time of our lives. You know those big 16-wheeler semis that kids try to get to blow their horns? Well, we got to actually blow the horns ourselves. Despite the fact that we may have had to sleep in the truck from time to time, it was still super cool as a kid. We also used to have fun and creative activities around the house. For example: we'd have treasure hunts for loose change in the house. And if we were really lucky, we'd get to go camping in the house. You know, that's when my parents would turn off the TV, all the lights and the heat, and we'd snuggle up in sleeping bags in the front room and pretend we were in the woods roughing it for a few days. Now that I have bills, I realize we just couldn't pay ours. I was bamboozled and loved every minute of it. Come to think of it, I still like camping today because of those experiences. I still love fishing too, I just didn't know when I was little we were actually catching our dinner, or we wouldn't eat. I guess as a kid I didn't know my story either.

What I do know is my story isn't over! Yes, God is still working on me and my legacy is being created as we speak. I will be a part of history, and it doesn't necessarily have anything to do with Thomas Jefferson, but for the simple fact that I'm living my life to the fullest right now. So many people think of Black History Month as just being about Martin Luther King Jr. and Rosa Parks, but it's about so much more. It's about our proud ancestors who were kings and queens, plus those who survived an unbearable trip across the ocean just to be put into a horrific life of slavery. Yes, it's about the march and the dream, but it's also about YOU and the fact that you're living history. You are the history people will be talking about in 50 years. What will they say about you?

Suited for Success

In my humble opinion, here are a few ways I think you can make the greatest impact on history or #YourStory:

#1- Like King, DREAM BIG! To do that, sometimes you've got to change your mindset. People say, "Don't get your hopes up. Maybe you should lower your expectations." Well, I'm here to tell you… get your hopes up! Expect God's best for your life!

I think a lot of times we block ourselves from achieving our goals because we're afraid to dream and fail. It's easy to look at the situation around you and say, "I'm never going to be able to make something of my life because I'm broke, not as pretty, as tall, or as smart" as someone else. Well, STOP. Stop focusing on what you think isn't working for you and either let it work for you or find the things that can work in your favor. Do you think super model Tyra Banks would be where she is if she let a big forehead stop her from dreaming big? What about media mogul Russell Simmons? If you've ever heard him talk, he has a lisp, but it never stopped him from making multi-million-dollar deals. How about President Barak Obama? People said we wouldn't have a black president in our lifetime. #YesWeCan. He didn't let the color of his skin or his ethnic sounding name stop him from dreaming. He didn't let the fact that there had never been a black president stop him from dreaming big. He didn't even let people that tried to take the job out from under him stop his dream. So, stop letting stuff, people, and negativity keep you from dreaming bigger than you could ever imagine. Don't listen to the haters that say no you can't, because like Obama, #YesYouCan!

I believe in speaking things into existence. If you want it to be true, speak it, and claim it now. Every great thing was created in the mind! Don't start defeating yourself by saying, "Well, I know it's probably not going to happen or it's not possible, but I want to be a doctor one day." NO, hold your head up high and say with confidence, "I'm going to be a doctor" (or whatever your dream is). Say it with conviction! Even if your dream is to buy a new home and you have $10.00 in your back account, still claim it like it is so. Don't let your current finances determine your future or hold you back from dreaming. So what if you're broke and you can't afford to go anywhere? You might as well start dreaming and formulating a plan to get you where you want to be. There are those who dream while sleeping and others who dream while awake. Which one are you? A dream without action is dead. That means you have to not only dream about it but believe in it. You have to put your mind where your mouth is and start taking actions to make your dream come true! If you want to be on TV one day, you can start now. Maybe that means start by reading the paper out load everyday like news anchors. Do the morning announcements at school or church, or maybe a web TV show, or finally start filling out college applications to universities with great TV degree programs. If you're young, take the adults in your life to task. It's their responsibility to help you get to where you want to go but remember they can't make it happen for you. You are the master of your fate. You are the captain of your soul. If it's a pro basketball player you want to be, that's great. But, like Jordan and LeBron say, "Practice makes perfect." So, you have to put the time in if you want results. It's not about what you do in season, it's about what you do in the off-season (your down time) that makes you successful! Are you sitting on the couch vegging out or are you running every morning, reading every morning, sharpening your mind, preparing your spirit? Now, while we're talking about being pro athletes, let me just remind you that I said dream big. Don't limit God's blessings in your life! Don't get to Heaven just to see all the doors He wanted to open for you! There are other options in sports than just playing on the team. Think about it, maybe you can coach, manage, or buy and entire team instead.

#2- Dare to be Different. Being different starts in the mind. What are you thinking? Train your brain to focus on things outside of your current circumstances. Maybe you have three kids, all by different men. That may be your story, but your sequel can be even better. It can be that you raised all those kids to be successful, and they went to college and became the next leaders of the world. Open your mind!

Maybe you never finished high school and are working at a fast-food restaurant. You're still living; that must mean your story is not over yet. There's still time to turn that situation around, get a GED, go to college, and buy several fast-food restaurants. The choice is up to you, so don't blame "the man" or your parents or a hard life. The only person you can blame is yourself!

Now parents, I'm going to get on you too. Help these kids. Even if they're not your kids, help them. It takes a village to raise a child. Nowadays, the villagers are afraid of the children. Take back your control. Let them know that you love them too much to see them go down the wrong path. Don't just look in the other direction. Don't be afraid that by disciplining them you will isolate them. If it is done out of love, there is no limit to where they can go. Sometimes we try to rule with an iron fist and say, "That kids is the devil, I don't know what's wrong with him. He's just stupid." But, you don't know their story. They may come from an abusive home, they may have a chemical imbalance, they may spend 90 percent of their day being called stupid, evil, and other horrible names, who knows? But what I do know is that if you tell them, "You're brilliant, you're beautiful, you can be anything you want to be, and I love you," that right there can change them and the world!

Now, young people, please don't be mistaken, this is not something for adults only. You all can do the same kind of positive reinforcement with your peers. With all the shootings going on in the schools, you'd think you would try to be nice to everyone. You may think it's funny to make fun of people, call them names or even bully them, but it's NOT! That's what cowards do so no one will make fun of them. It's what abused kids might do because hurt people hurt people. If you're really the tough guy or the coolest girl, then stand up for the kids that are getting picked on. Why not dare to be different? Why not put some peer pressure on other people to do the right thing? If nothing else—if that bullied kid comes to school with a gun, I bet they won't shoot the only person who cared about them and tried to help. Think about it.

#3- Make a Plan to get from point a to point b. Some people create vision boards, some make benchmark goals, others write lists. The point is, they put their vision to action by first dreaming it, then writing it down, and finally following their plan. In the Bible, Proverbs 29:18 (KJV) says: "Where there is no vision, the people perish." I've always found that it's easier to make my visions reality when God is a part of my journey. Just to be clear, that doesn't mean I'm always going to get what I want when I want it. But, if God is in it, even what I think are detours are really blessings to my life. So, I encourage you to get in the Word. Know what God says about you. Who are you? Whose are you? What are His promises over your life? What is His vision for you? What is your vision for yourself? I'm not being PC, I'm being real. I would be nothing without God, and I know it's only by His grace that I've come this far.

Where are you now? Write it down and be honest with yourself. Assess what skills you currently have and what skills you need. Where do you want to see yourself in one year, five years, ten years? What is your vision for your life? For your family? Now, how can you get from point a to point b? If you don't know, find someone who is doing what you want to do. Find out what their path was and ask them for advice. You'd be surprised what people will tell you if you just ask. Although all our paths are different, maybe they can provide insight into what you should be doing to get where you want to go.

The hardest part of planning for your future may be not making everyone you've known a part of it. If your friends are holding you back and are unwilling to go on the journey with you or support you, they've got to go! If it's family, don't spend so much time around them. I know that's easier said than done, but just because it's dark outside doesn't mean you can't let your light shine bright. Maybe, just maybe, some of your light will help them shine too. However, try to surround yourself with likeminded people—people who dream while awake, people who aren't afraid to be different, people who know God's Word and can encourage you when you don't have the strength to encourage yourself. Iron sharpens iron, so don't be afraid to be the dumbest person in the room. If you're fencing with a sword while your opponent has a wooden club, you're not going to grow. As I've said, no two people have the same story, but we can help one another along the journey. We can hold one another accountable. We can sharpen one another's skills. We can encourage one another!

As I close, I remind you…

Dream big. Dream beyond your current circumstances! If the dream is something you can achieve on your own, then God can't get the glory. He has so much in store for you and your life. Don't limit Him.

Dare to be different. God put the vision within you—not your mama, not your daddy, not your teacher—you! Not everybody's going to get it. Not everybody's going to be your cheerleader. Sometimes you've got to stand by yourself for your faith to grow. Trust God for the things unseen!

Make a plan. Put your thoughts into action. When you're asked what you did with the seeds God planted inside of you, what will you say? You can't blame "the man." You can't blame your friends. You can't blame your circumstance. You can't say that no one told you because you just heard my story. As long as we have air in our lungs, I know God is not through with us yet! If He is doing it for me, He can do it for you! Your story isn't over, so make the most of it!

Chapter 3

#EVERYBODYMatters

Charles A. Archer

Excerpt from Everybody Paddles: A Leaders Blueprint for Creating a Unified Team

When I became director of a large Brooklyn-based social service agency in 2006, I knew little about management. I was a lawyer and a lobbyist. In those roles, other people made the leadership decisions. I participated and watched, but I didn't have the final say. Suddenly, I was in charge and hundreds of employees looked to me to make the important decisions. I quickly began to learn management techniques on the job. I also discovered that most managers go through the same process. Getting an MBA is nice, but it does not really prepare anyone for the realities of day-to-day, real-life actions. As a result, I decided to find books that provided realistic guidelines for someone like me or, for that matter, any executive charged with providing leadership. But, I found very little. All of the management books offered advice, but not enough seemed connected to what really happens inside an organization or an office. That's why this book came to be written. *Everybody Paddles* examines all aspects of management, from creating the original vision to communicating it to your team, with practical guidelines based on real experiences. What I learned grew into guiding principles that have helped my agency grow and maintain its position as a model for other social service agencies throughout New York. These principles will also work for any executive in any industry. I'm a firm believer in sharing knowledge. Management is all about identifying important issues and making the best decisions. I hope this book is useful to CEO's and other managers who are striving to be better.

Building Consensus with the *Everybody Paddles* Concept

This is a book about team building and leadership. I had spent some time working on how to express these concepts in a clear, concise way when the solution came to me one day as I glanced at a magazine. I was attending a conference at the time, and at that point in the schedule we were supposed to be networking for the benefit not only of ourselves but also of our organizations. Somehow, the networking party just got out of hand. Things happen. So, I walked into a vacant room, sat down on a couch, and flipped through my phone messages. That's when I saw it: a photograph of a whitewater raft on the cover of a sporting magazine. There were five people in the raft as the river raged on, threatening to capsize them all. They were all leaning into their oars at the same moment, however, and were executing, as if in one complete, unified movement, a turn to avoid the face of a huge rock in front of them. The water parted in a V formation, splitting into two white jet streams, and all eyes were focused on the right-hand side. The intensity of their focus got to me, as well as the sense that they were all executing that one turn in total cooperation. No one was sloughing off—unlike the conventioneers at the raucous party outside. A life-or-death turn, executed perfectly, in unison, by five people. "Everybody Paddles" became my slogan from then on. (There's a saying in my office: "Charles is crazy. Don't get in his way when he is passionate about something!") This idea had captivated me. A few days later, I was back at The THRIVE Network (the nonprofit organization in

Brooklyn I co-founded in 1996, where we handle about $35 million a year in services for the disabled community), and I imagined paddles everywhere—all over the walls—as a symbol of this newfound image of unity. I found a store that sold me a bunch of paddles, and the next day I started nailing them to the walls. To this day, they cover the premises. A few days after that, I took a magic marker and walked around our space—a large floor in an old customs building near the Brooklyn waterfront—and started writing on the paddles: "Everyone Paddles in the Same Direction, at the Same Time, Toward the Same Goal." I see this as a process that goes far beyond my social service agency. There's no reason it can't include individual families as well as communities, cities, states, and countries. That's because "Everybody Paddles" represents a pattern of growth, development, and improvement that occurs when all participants work together for a common interest. This concept is very important today. As we all know, society is divided by economics, education, classism, ageism, gender differences, religion, and partisan politics. Despite these challenges, I believe there is opportunity for unity because everyone shares the desired outcome of benefiting from a common interest. It does take everyone working together to achieve a common goal. Yet, I also recognize that we are individuals. As a result, the "Everybody Paddles" concept would seem to contradict the American mantra of self-dependence and individualism. It doesn't. Let me explain why. Great thinkers have often stressed individuality. I love a famous quotation from Hillel—one of the greatest sages in Jewish history—that encapsulates so much of what I want to say in this book: "If I am not for myself, who will be? If I am only for myself, what am I? If not now, when?"

With this perfect wording, uttered in first-century Jerusalem, Hillel was saying what I had been thinking all the while as the CEO of a social service agency: Stand up for yourself. Take responsibility and act as if you are alone during the crucial fights and moments. But also, always remember that human beings need one another, and the other person is you. When individuals with integrity join together with others of equal stature, they can paddle forward in confidence, trusting one another, to achieve what they set out to accomplish. Hillel introduced the concept of individuality, getting people to think about who they were. But according to historian Jacob Burckhardt, it wasn't until the Late Middle Ages—toward the beginning of the Renaissance, the time of rebirth of Western culture—that the concept truly began to catch on. During the Middle Ages, the veil covering human souls was a cloth of faith, biases, ignorance and illusions… in so far as the human being was considered only as belonging to a race, a population, a party, a corporation, a family, or any other forms of community. For the first time, it was Italy that broke this veil and dictated the objective study of the State and other worldly things. This new way of considering, reality aside, further developed the subjective aspect and man became individual, spiritual, assuming his new status' consciousness. America was founded soon after the end of the Renaissance in Europe by bold individuals who dared to sail thousands of miles across dangerous seas to an unknown land. As a result, Americans have always prided themselves on rugged individuality and acclaimed anyone with that perceived personality. Mountain men and heroic soldiers Daniel Boone, Kit Carson, and Sergeant Alvin York come to mind. The concept is stressed in our times. Donald Trump, a somewhat controversial businessman and developer who has helped many people lead productive lives, said about leadership, "You are a one-man army," I agree. Yes, you are when you need to be. The promotion of individuality, however, is only a façade. The web that unites us becomes clearly visible during tragedies, such as: the terrorist attacks on September 11, 2001, or the Boston Marathon bombings on April 15, 2013. In both cases, communities around the country banded together to show their solidarity with the victims in each great city. The same thing happened during the Iranian hostage crisis in the late 1970s, when yellow ribbons served as the symbol of American unity. Our individual opinions and political differences were smoothed over by the desire to present a united front as Americans.

Americans may talk about I, but are acutely aware that the better pronoun is we. We often work as individuals in a group setting. That approach provides opportunities for creativity while helping the organization reach toward its goal. To promote this reality, I outline strategies that have been proven to modify attitudes, capabilities, and efforts, acknowledging that everybody within a given company must actively participate in the advancement of that company's mission, vision, value structure, and deliverables. To add practical experience to each principled approach, I have asked thought leaders and influencers to contribute their accounts of building consensus. These unique perspectives on the principles outlined in the book appear at the end of each chapter. By the time you have finished reading this book, you will have a blueprint for building and maintaining company consensus. You will know how to make sure that everyone on your team is inside the boat, paddling with singular focus toward the desired destination.

Principle One: Unity Stabilizes the Boat

Focusing on individuals who are building teams inside an organization raises two important questions: (1) What separates us? and (2) What brings us together? (The goal of the second question is so that we can work hard and achieve great things.) Every organization—whether a group, a company, an association, or any other entity that relies on the cooperation between its members—is simply a collection of individuals. As a result, the success of any organization depends totally on individuals. Obviously, most of us want to achieve success both on an individual and on a group level. We identify with success: Winning sports teams gain followers, for example. WE win, not just the team. An excellent organization has quality people who have been allowed over the course of their lives to develop great qualities like independence (responsibility), creativity (permissive flexibility), and accountability (getting the job done), but who can also cooperate and subordinate themselves when necessary to the mission at hand inside the organization. So, the core requirement of team building is a certain amount of freedom that both develops an individual and creates collective discipline. Unfortunately, not every organization can do that. With good leadership, any group of employees can learn to work together.

So, get ready, pick up your paddle, and start moving forward. Others will follow when everybody paddles.

Chapter 4

Faith. Grind. Inspire.

Dr. Jean Alerte

Someone asked me a few years back what three words describe what I do and who I am. I said, "Faith. Grind. Inspire." As a young entrepreneur for almost two decades, I have been through some storms but also seen way more sunny days. I have this mantra I say to myself all the time: "Every day, in every way, I get better and better and better." Legacy is what moves me. I remember when I was in high school I used to tell my classmates, "I'm going to inspire thousands of people to follow their dreams!" I have always had this passion to inspire people, to show them they don't have to be afraid of their dreams because regret is far worse than fear! Regret can't be fixed. That's why I love that every day I have the opportunity to work with youth and adults, pushing them to do the work they are striving toward. Funny enough, I have spent hours conversing with individuals about life, entrepreneurship, goal-setting, etc. It's second nature to me. The biggest adversity that I believe I faced, and anyone who is going for a major goal will face also, is self. Of course, you will have issues, hurdles, and different challenges, but the biggest struggle is internal! Limited belief is real, and once you can acknowledge that fact you will be in a much better place.

When I was 18 years old, I started working as a loan officer at a mortgage bank in Long Island, N.Y. I was super excited because I got to talk to people and help them achieve the American dream of home ownership, but I had a few struggles. One was my circle. No one understood why I didn't want a job that paid a salary. They told me I couldn't be successful in this industry because I was too young, I was a black boy on Long Island, I didn't look the part, and I didn't know what I was talking about. So, because of this, every time I heard a no, I ran to try to find a job. But, something inside of me never wanted to fully quit my position. I stuck it out and tackled the four limiting belief seeds that were planted in my young mind. I enrolled in a course that educated me on FHA loans and programs, read books, and traveled to seminars to master the products I was selling in the marketplace. I started going shopping for more suits and ties versus jeans and Timbs. I kept pushing during the process, and guess what? The potential clients I sat in front of didn't care about my age nor the color of my skin because I knew my product and I was confident on both the outside and the inside. My passion for my business grew so much that I moved up from team leader to branch manager and eventually to vice president of sales for the entire bank by the age of 23. I know I made it sound easy but trust me it took a lot of work and money! I actually hired a coach for $2,000.00 to keep me accountable! That's where I got the mantra: "Every day, in every way, I get better and better and better." My coach pushed me to face my fear of speaking to people. Growing up as a Haitian kid, it was disrespectful to look into the eyes of an adult when speaking to them. Once I got into the business world, I found out quickly that not looking into the eyes of a person you are trying to do business with is an indication that you are either not telling the truth or you're hiding something. My coach actually made me stand on Park Avenue in New York City, go up to random people and introduce myself. After the third person, the fear of regret and not trying became relevant. I urge you to ask yourself as you are reading this book, "Do I want success so badly that I would pay a consultant to help push me?" Would you take courses to make yourself more knowledgeable? What would you do to get better in your field? Would you get out of your own way to achieve success?

In 2007, I started my branding and advertising agency, ACA Branding Agency, in New York with a few of my friends. Due to the success I achieved in the banking industry, I was ready to tackle this one! We took NYC by storm. Call this part "Internship with the City." I treated it as an internship with the city because I wanted to work my way up and prove that we were great! We took on free projects with high profile celebrities, venues, and brands just to build our name and creditability. ACA found itself acquiring some of the biggest names in sports, fashion, and hospitality. By 2009, I was set to produce a comedy show with three comedians that at the time didn't have a spotlight on them! The goal was to put the show together to showcase the fact that we could promote, market, and obtain media coverage for an event. I talk more about this in my book *Do Right, Do Good*, but here I want to talk about the struggle. The headliner that I wanted to work with was Kevin Hart! I know you're saying, "That's an easy show, right?" Wrong. Like I said, this was 2009 and Kevin wasn't Kevin Hart. I had to convince his agent to give me an opportunity. I understood his concern because I had never put together a show with 3,000 seats. Ever! It took us four months of heavy promotion and rejection because people in this area had never seen Kevin do stand up. As I'm writing this, I'm thinking about how I really believed in ACA and what we were capable of!

Faith is one of the three words I said describe me. Now, let me explain something to you. No one will ever have more faith in your dreams and aspirations than you. Your friends and family might believe in you and see your vision, but if you are under the impression that they should push your dreams or business idea you're wrong! You sort of have to be obsessed with your vision. You should have a crystal-clear painting of your brand, book, restaurant, or whatever it is you are doing. Every time someone asks you about your project, you should light up so bright they need glasses! Faith and passion go hand in hand, and once you truly have complete confidence in yourself and your vision nothing can stop you! In my opinion, you can by nervous; but, when you start talking about your project, I should see another part of you!

We've talked about faith in yourself and in your project, now you might want to know how you can channel your energy. But, no one can help you with that! If you're doing something solely for money or fame, you won't last long. Sorry, but it's true. My suggestion is to set aside some time every day, when you're focused, and just sit still in silence. When I'm feeling overwhelmed or anxious, I take a break and mediate for 10 to 15 minutes. Russell Simmons introduced mediation to me in the book *Do You* back in 2009. I read it and I can truly say it works. I've told him thank you on various occasions and I will say it again! Mediation is truly not magic. Our lives are super busy with many moving parts to try to balance. The feelings we deal with are normal. When you let your ideas, to-do list, issues, and random thoughts settle, you will find that the emptiness is peace. There you might be able to see what your true passions are.

We've talked about faith, now let's talk about grind. This word has been thrown around for years, and I think for some it's watered down. When I hear the word grind, I get excited! I get pumped and ready to put in work! Grind is the effort you put toward your particular project. I can give hours of grind stories because I put in the work every day and growing up it's what I saw in my father. I was taught that if you want something of great importance, you must work to obtain it. I grinded every day in the mortgage industry. At first, it was to pay for college; but, it turned into something bigger. I grinded because I wanted to inspire the younger generation. I wanted to succeed to prove to myself I could do it and to make enough so that I could set myself up for the next moves.

When you say grind, you cannot forget about work ethic. Let's break down those two words. The definition of work is: activity involving mental or physical effort done in order to achieve a purpose or result. Ethics is: a set of moral principles, especially ones relating to or affirming a specified group, field, or form of conduct (Oxford Dictionary). So, when you put both words together, it's going to mean different things to different people. But at the end of the day, to achieve a goal you must have some form of work ethic. The other day, I was talking to one of my clients' sales guys and I asked him what his monetary goal was for the year. It took him two seconds to give me the number. Then, I asked him the question I want you to ask yourself. Are you grinding daily to achieve that number? Better yet, do you think you will achieve that number based on your current work ethic and grind? If you want help, let me add some value by sharing what I do to ensure that I hit my numbers or achieve my goals.

First, be consistent! Be accountable for your words. If you say you will be somewhere at a certain time, be there. As an entrepreneur, all we really have is our reputation (which now is being called your brand). Second, prepare the night before. Take some time, either before you go home or before you go to sleep, to write down everything productive you must complete the following day. This one tip has helped so many people achieve a bit more success. The person who prepares the night before has the upper hand and can tackle the day more successfully. Do a bit more than you are required to do! If you're supposed to make 10 visits a day, try to get 12 visits in. If you have a goal of engaging with 15 new people a week on social media, shoot for 20. My mentor taught me, "Do it now." Get it done now while it's fresh on your mind. "Oh, I have to call so and so." Ok, call now. If someone is referring you or you are referring someone, share the info now. Don't wait because you will forget. While getting it done now, preparing the night before, doing more, and being consistent, you must drop perfection! You must focus on the process and not the result. The process is the fun, the process is the grind! There I go with that word again, but it's true! Don't think everything you do will be perfect! I lost a lot of money, but that was the cost of learning, growing, and failing my way up to achieving my goals.

Now, this next one is probably not going to sit well with some, but I have to say it! When you're working, stay off of social media. If that's your job to post content and you're getting paid to be on there, I'm not talking to you. Continue to get that money. I'm talking to the people who during the middle of a workday, with a long to-do list, decide that the best option is to check Facebook and Instagram stories. You must cut out the distractions, whatever they might be. Sometimes the distraction might be your spouse or someone you just started dating. They have free time, so they just assume because you work for yourself you are free all day. You have to have that tough conversation with your friends, family, or whomever you let believe it was ok to call you during your workday to talk about last nights' shows, what bars are popping this coming weekend, or what's new on *Power*. Don't get me wrong, these conversations can happen, just not during your productive hours.

Lastly, locate people who you consider running mates. They don't have to work with you directly, but they are grinding on their own visions. This connection is important because like the saying goes, "Swords sharpen swords." So, hang around people who can sharpen you and vice versa. My wife and I have been sharpening each other for the past 12 years and it's simply because we share the same vision about what we want for our family. I cannot tell you how blessed I am to have a wife that understands me and supports my vision. Most of my success would not have been possible if it weren't for her support. If you currently don't surround yourself with people who can sharpen you, then I suggest you go network, join committees, or find someone you feel you can add value to and reach out to them.

Have faith in your vision, grind on your vision, and eventually you will inspire individuals in your circle, your community, or the world (especially now because of social media). Your grind in Deer Park, N.Y. or Atlanta, Ga. can inspire individuals in India or Brazil. Inspiring is the legacy! Your efforts will inspire someone else to follow their vision. The way to make a community flourish is to inspire the people. The weight of regret is far heavier than the weight of fear. By putting in the work, you will fuel people as I hope my words today have fueled you! God bless!

Chapter 5

Full Circle

Jamael Thompson

My story starts when my parents decided to allow me to attend private school (nursery through eighth grade) at our church instead of going to neighborhood public schools in Brooklyn, New York. This decision changed my life forever which is the reason for the title full circle. As the youngest of three, I'm assuming my parents thought to themselves, "Why not pay for private school education?" When you think of a private school, most people think of some suburban area, different cultures, and rich kids. Not in my case. My private school was in East New York, Brooklyn, across the street from project buildings near Linden Blvd. Imagine wearing a uniform (brown and yellow) everyday, while your friends are wearing the hottest gear and freshest sneakers. Also, being so close to the projects neighborhood meant that guys would rob, jump, and pick on the corny private school kids. Thankfully, I lived in the projects, so I was familiar with a lot of the neighborhood guys. That made my time there easier than most in my school. Walking to and from school always seemed to be an adventure because there were other schools within that two to three block radius. But, once we entered our gates, I felt safe. The education I received from this small, church-affiliated private school was bar none. Most of my classmates read three or four grades above our level and we focused on Math, Science, Social Studies, and Language Arts. We didn't realize that our level of education was better than most of our peers in our neighborhood.

Things were good until we moved from Linden Project Apartments to a house with three bedrooms, one and a half bathrooms, a basement, and a garage, on the other side of East New York near New Lots Ave. You would think we were moving on up, huh? Not at all. It was the 90s in East New York, Brooklyn. I remember moving in and going across the street to the neighborhood corner store to find one or two bags of chips, old milk, half empty shelves, and realizing this isn't a corner store. It was always dark in there and only got busy at night. I quickly realized we lived across the street from "The Spot" (an illegal drug location). Even though we lived in a house, it felt safer when we lived in the projects. I remember during the night, when my father left for work, random people would ring the doorbell asking for things like money, to use the bathroom, and to use our phone. It was crazy in the early years. My room was in the front of the house, so I would always hear arguing and fighting. One memory that sticks out from those early years was a woman overdosing in front of our house. It was a daily occurrence to see crack valves laying around and drug users walking around asking for money. It was sad to see the deterioration of regular people after being hooked on drugs. I especially remember seeing a gentleman who had a good job and family lose everything because of doing drugs. He was one of my guiding examples of what I didn't want to be, and I used that to push me.

After our move, I was still able to attend the private school, but my 10-minute walk turned into 10-15-minute ride on two buses. Then, I had to walk a couple blocks which isn't bad, but in a brown and yellow uniform it felt like an eternity. At first, my sister (who was five years older than me) would take me to school because her school was down the block from mine. But, once she graduated and went to high school, I was on my own. Imagine a nine-year-old kid in a uniform, riding two buses, and walking to school. It wasn't fun. However, I loved my school and the administrators who pushed us to be great no matter the circumstances. The sentiment resounded through the private school that since our parents decided to sacrifice something to allow us to attend, we couldn't and shouldn't take their sacrifice lightly. I remember having competitions in school to get the best grades in class. But, I was one of the cool kids, so I couldn't be the best or I would lose my reputation. I would always do enough to stay a B or B+ student, but with a little more effort I could have easily been an A student. I loved being a cool kid. We sat in the back of the bus on trips and chilled with the pretty girls in school. School was my saving grace, but East New York was East New York. Thankfully, my parents were God-fearing people, and because of their prayers I was always placed in the best situations growing up.

Since it was still a bad area of Brooklyn in the late 90s, I never left my block. There was a public park across the street called Elton Park, but drug users and drug dealers resided there. I met all the neighborhood kids in the notorious 75th. Precinct Summer Camp, which allowed me to befriend guys

I would never have had the chance to because we were on different paths in life. These friendships allowed me to bypass the traditional rite of passage (selling drugs) in my neighborhood because they wouldn't allow me to entertain the idea. Upon graduating from eighth grade in 1996, I was afforded an opportunity to attend a private high school similar to the one I described earlier—rich kids, beautiful campus, and different ethnicities. But, my parents said no. My only option, since I didn't get into a specialized school, was to attend my zone school, Thomas Jefferson High School. At the time, Thomas Jefferson was probably one of the worst schools in Brooklyn. I wasn't feeling that option. Thankfully, my private school administrator took me to Boys and Girls High School in Bed-Stuy and managed to get me into the Honors Program due to my grades. As I mentioned previously, God has always allowed me to be in the best situation. He allowed me to go from one of the worst schools in Brooklyn to one of the best. Again, school was a haven as Bed-Stuy (affectionately known as "Do or Die Bed-Stuy") wasn't a great area of Brooklyn. Honors Program pushed me to another level because like my old private school, we had competitions to get the best grades. Some classmates were removed or left, but those that persevered were afforded the best education.

Once I left school, however, my journey home was another adventure on the C train. In the late 1990s and early 2000s, gang violence started to be prevalent in Brooklyn, especially Bloods and Cribs. I remember seeing kids getting jumped, faces slashed, robberies, etc. on several occasions. Riding the train home during those times was trying, especially watching 20-30 kids walking through subway cars looking for trouble. I remember when about 20 kids jumped a boy sitting right next to me because he was from a different set. I used school as a means to stay out of trouble, so I would attend travel club meetings or just chill with my teachers and friends.

Choosing the right friends is a major component to building your success. Most of my friends were the smart kids. Getting in trouble wasn't cool in our inner circle. We all had aspirations to be successful, so we took full advantage of our education. In Honors classes, you had to maintain a certain grade point average and teachers had to recommend that you continue. My sophomore year, when I was still trying to straddle the line between cool kid and smart kid, my English Honors teacher removed me from the class (due to my comedic behavior) and placed me in a regular English class. On the first day of this regular English class, my teacher was explaining subject, verb, and predicate sentences. The spelling words were cat, hat, and mat. I realized how advanced I was compared to students who weren't in Honors class; I had learned that topic in elementary school. After that experience, I worked hard to maintain my Honors status as it was a privilege not a right.

High school was great, but during these years from 14 to 18 years old, a lot of my "friends" made some life-changing decisions and fell into the typical inner-city black kid pitfall. The drug game in the hood is an easy proposition for a lot of these guys. All they see is the money, the nice clothes, the hottest sneakers, and the pretty girls. Consequences aren't taken into consideration at that age. Thankfully, I always saw the end game for my life, which didn't include getting caught up in the drug game. As an honors student, I knew my path was bright because I worked hard, and I was determined to be successful. One of my best attributes was my sense of humor, which allowed me to be down with the cool kids and not sacrifice my drive to be a good student. Oddly enough, my guidance counselor mentioned my ability to straddle the line between cool and smart.

College was an interesting experience in Buffalo, N.Y. (which is about eight hours from Brooklyn). I decided to travel outside of my comfort zone for school. In Brooklyn, there weren't a lot of opportunities to interact with individuals of different races, so I used college as my spring board. College was also where I fell in love with business, which ultimately led to my degree in economics. During my time in college, I made it a point to visit my old private school to have conversations with the seventh and eighth graders. I felt it was my obligation to give back in that capacity. My perspective has always been that this world is bigger than your block or neighborhood. A lot of inner-city kids never left their neighborhoods, and I wanted to broaden their tunnel vision mentality. So, every year during my breaks, I went back to the school and spent some time with the youth. Ironically, this constant trip back to my old school led to my start in banking. Due to the relationships I had with the administrators, they gave me a great recommendation with a small regional bank. I used this opportunity to build my career. I worked hard to be my very best by learning and comprehending various aspects of banking. Being successful has always been a driving force because of the amount of failure I saw around me in my neighborhood.

Suited for Success

I started out in the management training program and within six months I was promoted to branch supervisor with the least amount of experience in my branch. Only a year into the role, I was promoted to assistant branch manager then asked to manage another location in Manhattan considered one of the worst branches for our region. Within one year at my new location, we changed the narrative and became a high performing branch due to our hard work and drive. Twelve, going on thirteen, years in the Banking industry (currently a vice president in business banking) has been an awesome journey and every day is a new opportunity to build my relationships and networks. One of my favorite quotes is: "Excellence costs more but it pays for itself." I live by this mantra in my quest to be successful.

Chapter 6

Achieve Your Version of Success
Aaron S. Jenkins

Knowing what success means to you is what makes the difference. It all culminates into what will eventually be your contribution to this human experience.

Struggle and Adversity

In my high school years, I was often afforded the opportunity to lead and encourage others. I was hired to work with my peers as the director of recreation at the neighborhood YMCA, while simultaneously doing music and community outreach throughout New York. Whether it was music and producing or helping community youth like myself, I struggled to understand that mentorship and counseling could be a way of life. My greatest challenge had become my inability to pinpoint a specific area of interest to focus my efforts. When your interests and capabilities take you in multiple directions, it can be quite a challenge locking in a specific goal or purpose. So, I found myself being happy with the work but not with the money I was making. It was hard to make sense of the fact that in order to afford the type of life I wanted to live, I was going to have to find different work. I was young, but I still had a vision of what I wanted my life to look like. So, in between being away at school and going home, I tried my hand at working for different corporations like IBM, Kinney Shoe Corp., and UPS. I eventually landed on Wall Street. I found I was enjoying the money, but not the work. The work took away from what I really loved to do.

Ask Questions

As a teenager, I often wondered why some people seemed to have more than others. I found it interesting that there were people that had so much promise and others that seemingly found good luck wherever they went. I thought the difference maker was work ethic, but I was wrong. Relationships were what helped set me on the right path. Growing up in Bed-Stuy, Brooklyn, whether you talked a good game or not, your respect was earned by what you produced. Sure, there were those that seemed to have all the favor in the world, but in the end, we all become products of what we think about the most. It took some time, but through reading and surrounding myself with people that were smarter than me, I had no choice but to mature. I asked questions of myself when I missed the mark or goal I was shooting for. Because of my youth, I often wrestled more with the questions than the solutions. Overall, I was willing to do the work! If it was basketball related, I attempted to work harder by asking Coach Brown, "Can I stay in the gym after practice to get up more shots?" If it was musical, I spent late nights and weekends reading and collaborating with my partners that had the same passion. As I grew older, I used the same formula. If it was mentorship, I sat with my elders as often as I could to glean an understanding of how to better manage my relationships.

Pursue What Makes You Happy

I remember really having a passion to pursue community outreach through music and public speaking. I once attempted to start a nonprofit organization with a few partners. We gathered information, met weekly, and pushed forward to pursue a goal that would cause us to stretch beyond our limited knowledge and resources. I must say, those days were well spent. In hindsight, they were priceless moments that taught me a lot about myself and having expectations of others. We came up with some really good ideas in hopes of influencing the communities within New York City and eventually throughout the tri-state area. We sat in meetings with the local assemblyman and senator to gain their support. Our efforts were proof positive that we were onto something major. Over time, plans changed, and we ended up going our separate ways. But, the spark that was ignited within me for community outreach never died. By now, the dots were connecting for me—the good ideas, the shared vision, and the passion for people. All the components were working together in such a way that landed me back in school for my master's degree. As I stepped out of my comfort zone, everything began falling into place more than ever before. Relationship after relationship aligned me with information and the opportunities to accomplish my goals every step of the way. Currently, with over 20 years of experience in counseling, public speaking, community outreach, and partnerships, the future remains bright and the possibilities are endless!

Life Lessons

I must say that throughout my journey, I've been blessed to be around some good people. I've had several pivotal moments that taught me the priceless gift of relationships and the importance of staying connected. You never know when your vision will provide energy for someone else's vision and vice versa. This is why it is imperative that we maintain the big picture; we all need each other. As much as we might want to be independent from others, stand alone, and seemingly remain untouchable, the idea of separatism is what causes a lot of failed partnerships. Take for example the thought of being in a race. You're lined up on the track, awaiting the referee's gun to go BANG! When you take off, your competitors run in the opposite direction. At that moment, what do you do? Do you change your course and follow the crowd, or do you stay on track running your race? What I have found is that as you continue doing what you're supposed to do, you will see the results. There will be shortcuts for whatever you plan to accomplish in life, but are you willing to dig deep within to endure the overbearing persecution that comes from those you pass along the way? You see, while running your race, doing things the right way may not always seem worth it (especially considering the banter you experience from those doing things their way and seemingly achieving success a lot quicker). The goal is to remain consistent, work hard on yourself, and continue doing your due diligence to finish your race!

Three Steps to Achievement

#1: Don't Fear Being Alone

In order to finish your race, there will be moments when you feel alone. Don't run from these opportunities, embrace them. Remember that relationships are like modes of transportation. Some take you where you need to go, and others take you further away from your destination. Choose wisely! The relationships that help you the most could come from people you have never known. Don't be afraid to enter the room by yourself and come out with a team behind you.

#2: Pay Attention to Details

Know that every decision you make will be one that you're willing to own. It's in owning your choices that you will take the proper precautions. Consider how today's car services and taxis have become more intricate—describing the driver, make, model, and color of the vehicle with hopes to ensure you reach your desired destination without confusion. It's in the details that these companies have revolutionized the transportation industry. Would you willingly get into a cab traveling to an unknown destination? That would be absurd for someone that values their time. In the same way, why would you allow casual relationships to take you places that aren't in the direction of your goals? Stay focused!

#3: Be GREATful (misspelled on purpose)

When it comes to achieving success, I try to maintain an attitude of gratitude. For me, being great requires gratefulness. Each interaction stands the possibility of being different from the norm. There have been moments when I've been able to learn a lot more from others, even in my attempts to assist them through their journey. As individuals, we can often sense when a person is being sincere and genuine. So, the more you remain upfront, personable, and gracious, the more others will reciprocate with the same sincerity. Of course, there will be those that challenge your professionalism, but don't allow the small percentage that bring entropy to disrupt your positive energy. Don't let negative people change you into who they are.

If I Could Do it

Looking back, if I had to do it all over again, I'm sure I would have done some things differently. For one, I would have asked myself the question, "Why not?" more often. I have found that when faced with that question in recent years, it gave me the courage necessary to do the hard work required to achieve the goals I had laid out before me. Overall, I understand that I am who I am today because of my experiences, so I wouldn't change too much of what I've been through.

Connect the Dots

No matter what you're going through, consider the process you're experiencing. Ask questions during that process that will help you gain clarity; assume nothing. Although you may find yourself in a challenging place, remember you're going through it all for a reason. The reason may not make sense right now, but when it does you will be a master at what you do. Allow your experiences, both good and bad, to arm you with the know how to encourage others along their journey of life and success. Success is not always about having a lot of money but being successful at what you do can make a lot of money for you. Remain optimistic. Charisma can open doors for you just because you have the right energy. Every door might not be the door for you but remember to take note because the lesson you learn could be for someone else you come across. The relationships you encounter can build synergistic bonds for the future. You never know when you'll need to connect individuals that can assist each other toward their pursuit of vision and purpose. My success has been in knowing that life does make sense, especially helping others to discover THEir (done purposely) truth. Life has many roads that can take you in many directions, but if you are willing to find and embrace truth it will always lead you to success.

Chapter 7

Let Your Situation Be Your Motivation

Randall E. Toby

It was just a little past three in the afternoon when my younger brother, Glenn, and I reached our Brooklyn home right after finishing school that day. We were in elementary school at the time, so just like many parents often do, our mother provided us with our own set of keys to let ourselves into the apartment since she couldn't afford a babysitter. However, something was just a little different that day. Although I was young, I still knew that seeing a bright-colored note on our apartment door wasn't a good sign. My mother had lost her job which affected her ability to continue to pay rent. Eventually, that led to our family being evicted from our Brooklyn apartment at 1470 Sterling Place. I was raised by a single mother who is a brave, kind, intelligent, and generous woman. She was suffering from mental illness and was later diagnosed with paranoid schizophrenia, a form of mental illness which can cause frequent paranoid delusions and auditory hallucinations (seeing and hearing things that are not there). It's a severe chronic disease that affects approximately one percent of the population. Without a place to stay, our family packed as many clothes as we could into three large brown suitcases and took the number two train toward downtown Brooklyn where we settled in on a hard-wooden bench located inside the Atlantic Terminal Station. It was called Flatbush Avenue back then and is a stop along the Long Island Railroad's Atlantic Branch.

We spent the next two weeks eating and sleeping there as we watched commuters, not even aware of our existence, go about their daily travels to and from work each day. I felt invisible. As we sat there, I wondered to myself why no one asked us if we were hungry. Why didn't they check to see if we needed help? Or had they even asked themselves, "Who are those people?" These were just some of the questions that came to mind during that time. But, we were not alone. Research shows that as recently as March 2017, there were 61,936 homeless people in New York State, including:

15,525 families and 23,445 children in New York City alone. Many people view the homeless as a group of crazy people simply reaping the outcome of making a lifetime of bad decisions, individuals taking advantage of federal benefits, or a stubborn kid that just didn't want to listen to their parents. However, some of the major causes of homelessness include overcrowded housing, job loss, domestic violence, hazardous housing conditions, or even military veterans suffering from PTSD (Post Traumatic Stress Disorder). Many people are not aware that people who are homeless often feel isolated, experience incredible stress, suffer from depression, or even look at themselves as being worthless.

It took several years before my family finally had a place to call our home again. During our transition, we spent time at our aunt's house in St. Albans, Queens, we were residents of the St. George Hotel in Brooklyn (which was often referred to as a welfare hotel), and we even spent a few months in a family shelter provided by public assistance. There were times that some of the other children my brother and I met during our travels saw my mother's erratic behavior and referred to her as being crazy. Those words pierced my soul. Children can be ruthless and cruel sometimes, and due to their youth and lack of understanding they are often unaware of how their words can damage or hurt someone. Over time, my mother's condition worsened to the point that she was admitted into Creedmoor Psychiatric Center (a mental institution located in Queens, New York) for several months. We visited her on several occasions, not quite understanding why our beautiful and loving mother was strapped to a chair and barely coherent due to the various drugs they used to treat her. I asked myself, "Could this be the same woman that took my brother and I to the American Museum of Natural History, Haden Planetarium, Bronx Zoo, and local concerts so that we would experience different cultures, broaden our minds, and be exposed to some of life's small treasures?" My mother was always so poised. She was one of the first African American women ever to be hired by the New York Telephone Company because of her impeccable style, grace, and the ability to articulate and present herself well. Looking back now, I often tell people that being homeless was one of the best things that ever happened to me. It is where I developed my life's motto and personal strategy for success, "Let your situation be your motivation." You must learn to channel those defining and often difficult moments that shape your life because they can be used as the fuel that ignites your comeback. Understanding how to control anger, disappointment, and pain to propel yourself to greatness is key. I believe that I have become a better man through self-discovery. I realize that every challenge, pain, disappointment, and failure you endure is a lesson that is part of God's bigger plan. I'm far from perfect, but I strive every day to be a little better than I was the day before.

I have learned to be comfortable with being uncomfortable. Allowing myself to let my situation be my motivation has deep meaning to me because I discovered that many of my difficult times often began as a burden but ended up being my testimony. Those times gave me the strength to encourage others. Sometimes you can become so attached to negative situations that you become focused on them. This type of mindset will continue to make you feel lost, devastated, and cause you to allow the situation to define who you are. This can keep you living in the past and not allow you to move forward. Focus instead on the process: What are you motivated by that can drive you toward your desired outcome? What are your dreams and goals? Are the steps you're taking toward your goal in line with the things you want to do or have? When you are growing, learning, and moving closer to your values and passions, time won't be wasted; it will be a life well lived regardless of your past. When your process aligns with your purpose, you'll succeed in a variety of ways. If you make God a priority in your life, He will reveal to you (in time) just how those difficult moments you face will shape your life forever and often lead you to discover your purpose.

Your problems will affect you in one of two ways: they will either make you bitter or force you to be better. A bitter person is someone who consistently complains about every barrier they face in life. Bitterness can make you become the kind of person other people don't want to be around. It's also vital for you to not be around people that are negative because they have a way of keeping you in a bad place. Life often sends us exactly what we put out; so, if you want good energy from others, give good energy to others. I've found that those who complain the most about the bad energy of others are often surrounded by it themselves. If this is a frequent problem in your life, it may be time to change the people who are in your circle. But, it all begins with you. Take a closer look at yourself in the mirror and do a self-assessment. Are you the kind of person that always expects the worst to happen? If so, I want you to know that it's never too late to change. It's simpler than you think.

Start feeding yourself positive information. When a person is hungry, they typically have a meal, which may consist of meat or fish, a vegetable, and a starch. Just like you feed your body, your mind requires food too! Everything you watch on television, the books you read, your choice of music, or the video games you play send positive or negative images and information that resonates within your mind and spirit.

I want to share with you some of the other valuable lessons gained from my past experiences: 1) Never become too attached to material possessions because they can be taken away at any time, 2) Family is the foundation of one's life, and 3) I'm actually much stronger than I ever thought I was. Whether you're a former drug addict, have been incarcerated, survived physical abuse, lost a good paying job, or are moving forward after a terrible relationship, you have more control over your life than you think! Everyone will face challenging situations that seem impossible to overcome, but picture yourself as a boxer training for a championship fight. The fight is life. You now have the courage, strength, and endurance to withstand some of life's hardest blows. Bad times either make you mad or magnificent, BUT the choice is always YOURS.

If you want to be the champion of your life, you must first train yourself to have a growth mentality and learn to control your emotions. You can start by creating a personal vision that should include your short-term goals (six months to a year) and long-term plan (which can be up to five years), then work on ways to execute your goals. Something I want you to keep in mind is that healing is a process and it will happen in its own time. You can't always rush through it. The way one person overcomes a bad experience is different from everyone else. To get through it, you must let yourself experience those feelings that come naturally. It doesn't matter if those feelings are grief, shock, or anger. You can move past bad experiences, but you must allow your emotions to adjust. Letting yourself feel is a part of your natural healing process. As you grow, you will suddenly realize that complaining does nothing to fix your problems. For example, instead of yelling at the waitress for adding pickles on your hamburger, be grateful that you have something to eat. Don't complain that you're having a bad day; instead, be grateful that you are still alive and breathing. Stop saying, "I hate my job," when there are so many people unable to find employment. Do something about it! Regardless of what you are facing, choosing to be negative isn't going to help your situation at all. Life will continually present you with negative situations, the key is how you adapt, persevere, survive, and ultimately learn a life lesson. It's YOU who has the power to choose how you react. Rather than waste energy and your reputation by reacting negatively, learn to turn a negative situation into a positive one. Don't let the actions of others or circumstances cause you to focus on the dark side. "Let your situation be your motivation" reminds me that my failures and disappointments have not only given me the fuel to overcome my setbacks, but they have also built up a deep reservoir of resilience in me (like an antidote or vaccine) that I can use against future challenges. Experiencing homelessness has turned out to be the greatest personal trainer of my life.

If you are wondering how my experiences shaped me in other ways, here are some examples. I am very empathetic and hate to see others go through what I've been through. They taught me how to be kind and to never underestimate someone else's pain, especially if I haven't gone through it myself. They provided me with wisdom. Little things don't bother me anymore. My pain made me look at life differently, and helped me to understand its true essence and appreciate the small things. I no longer seek to be happy because happiness is based on external conditions such as: how much money you have in the bank, the type of car you drive, the brand of clothes you wear, or perhaps the value of your home. Happiness is based on emotions and is temporary. Instead of happiness, being joyful is what I strive for. It's a state of mind and it has nothing to do with how you feel because it comes from deep inside of you. I value and cherish my relationships more. I realize that you have people you can lean on in times of trouble, and people who genuinely love you and are happy to support you. Pain makes you strengthen the bond between you and your closest friends and family. My pain has been my main inspiration to become an entrepreneur, professional speaker, start an organization (the Magnificent Men Mentoring Group), and even to write. How do you get started? Work on you:

- **Wake Up Early!**

Operate as though someone is working to take everything that you own.

- **Meditation or Prayer**

First thing in the morning, prepare your mind for obstacles that will surely come your way throughout the course of the day.

- **Read!**

Consistently have a thirst and hunger to improve, gain knowledge, or stay informed of any trends in your business, industry, or even current events

- **Build Powerful Relationships**

Surround yourself with people who want more out of life, are likeminded, and who are on the same path. They should be innovators, thinkers, and listeners who want to create change and leave a footprint in their lives as well as yours. They are willing to help others before helping themselves.

- **Be Determined**

Great leaders see things through to completion. They simultaneously track what may appear to be insignificant details and keep the larger picture in mind. They monitor anything they believe helps them achieve their goals. They don't give up easily when things don't go their way.

- **Create Balance in Your Life**

It is essential to maintain quality in life and work in order to be whole and in harmony. Your life is made up of many vital areas including: health, family, financial, intellectual, social, career, spiritual, recreational, personal growth, and romance.

- **Have a Plan**

Going through life without having goals is like taking a cross country road trip without a map or GPS. By designing a plan, you're less likely to be thrown off course when issues arise. A plan helps you to stay focused when there are distractions. Rarely does life go as you expect it to. Timing is everything. You must trust the universe that everything happens for a reason, because it does.

If you're wondering how my mother is doing after all these years, she's doing well. She moved to Atlanta, Georgia, where she lives with my sister, Judy, and assists with raising her grandchildren. She hasn't shown any signs of mental illness in over 20 years. Perhaps what my mother experienced wasn't just for her but was meant for me as well. I know that if I didn't face so many challenges in my life, I wouldn't be on my way to becoming the man God intended for me to be when I was born. Whatever the reason, I am grateful!

Chapter 8

I Am Not a Bastard

Dr. Oliver T. Reid

You're not what you've touched or what has affected you, but you are imprinted by what you hold on to.

Like over 72 percent of African American children living in the United States (statistic as of 2016), I was born out of wedlock and raised mostly by my single mother. After 21 hours of life-threatening and excruciating labor resulting from breech birth complications, I was born at 4:00 a.m. on September 25, 1976. My mother told me later that upon delivery, I slipped through both the doctor's and labor nurse's hands, nearly crashing head first onto the floor. Just in the nick of time, the labor nurse pulled me up by my wrist, leaving me in the squatting position with my feet lodged to the floor and my hands lifted. Little did I know that this bizarre sequence of events would serve as a prophetic omen for the way my life would unfold. Because of the trauma experienced at childbirth, I was placed inside a neonatal incubator under doctors' care for two weeks. For my survival and safety, it was important to maintain my environment with precise temperature, humidity, and oxygen concentration levels.

I learned later that my biological father, who had persistently tried to talk my mother into aborting me, arrived at the hospital intoxicated and walked into our hospital room. The word father is defined by The Free Dictionary as: "a man who creates, originates, or founds something." In stark contrast to that definition, here are the first words that proceeded out of my biological father's mouth: "This baby is not my son. His complexion is too light, and he doesn't look like me at all!" By anyone's definition, those are not the words of a true father. Although I couldn't comprehend the depth of the words my father had spoken over me, his spoken words would nonetheless create a gaping hole within the framework of my life. My father's initial spoken words released the spirit of denial over my life and sent me spinning helplessly on the Ferris wheel of rejection. Shortly after being discharged from the hospital, my mother ended her relationship with my father, and I had little or no contact with my dad for many years. Before long, my mother was introduced to another man by a mutual family member. Following several months of dating, he proposed to take my mother's hand in marriage, pledged his undying love for both my mother and me, and vowed to embrace me like his very own son. Determined to rebound from the rejection of her first love, and battling internal apprehension, she accepted his proposal. Without a moment's pause, they were married by a justice of the peace, and we all moved to another city to begin a brand-new life together. Unlike most dramas played out on the big screen, there were no scenes in my life that depicted living "happily ever after." Several years after moving to a neighboring city, my mom gave birth to her second child, and my life immediately took a turn for the worse. My stepfather, the only father figure I had known, began to resent me, and verbally lashed out at me. Before the age of five, I was called lazy, hardheaded, stupid, and crazy. And those were the good days. From the age of six until I turned twelve, my stepfather's rage intensified, and abusive words were now matched by physical blows to my frail body. The rooms in my inner-city project served as my personal war zone. Day after day, and night after night, I found myself helpless and painfully trapped behind enemy lines within my own home. As the years of my childhood passed me by, I grew more accustomed to being my stepfather's punching bag. He often came home mad at the world, and for no apparent reason punched me in the face until my nose started bleeding. Often during the beatings, my stepdad would grab both of my ankles and dangle me upside down until I wet my clothes in fear. Then, he would continue to beat me until he got tired and I could no longer cry. Nonetheless, I still yearned for my stepdad to embrace me as a son, and to feel a father's touch. I was well-acquainted with the love of a God-fearing mother but had never felt the embrace of a father. Despite the verbal and physical abuse, I still reached out to my stepfather for love and affirmation, only to have my heart crushed time and time again. The last time my stepfather physically abused me, the pounding was so severe that the scars are still tattooed on my body. At this point, my mother finally had enough and separated from my stepfather for several months.

Throughout the six month separation, my mother continued to pray and speak the prophetic Word of God over my life. Shortly after we moved into my Godmother's apartment, we began praying and calling out to God for healing and restoration.

Suited for Success

I will never forget feeling the presence of the Holy Spirit as I called out to God to become my father for the first time. So many times in my childhood, I cried out to God for help from my beatings, rejections, and pain, but this time I embraced God as my father. Instantly, at the age of twelve, God answered my call, filled me with His precious Holy Spirit, and became the father I was longing for my entire life. Then, God whispered to my spirit these six words that would transform my life forever: "My son is not a bastard." Immediately, I knew and understood that despite how badly I had been broken, God could still repair me. From the day I embraced God as my father, I was given an internal peace and eternal affirmation from the Holy Spirit that I would rise above all of my afflictions. God began to reveal to my mother and me that the sequence of events at my birth prophetically symbolized my life, and regardless of how severe the challenges were, I would always land on my feet with my hands raised toward Heaven.

After six months, my mother returned home and the physical abuse from my stepfather stopped. However, the mental and verbal abuse intensified and continued until I left home for college. Some years later, my stepfather was killed in a car accident. Just like that, without notice, he was gone.

Despite many opportunities, my stepfather never did muster up the courage to apologize to me for the many years of abuse. Through much travail, God granted me the grace to forgive my stepfather for all of his abuse, despite the fact that he died without reconciling or taking responsibility for his actions. I am a living witness that Romans 8:28 is not just a biblical cliché, for truly all things good, bad, and ugly work together for good for those who love God and are called according to His purpose.

After creating a strong relationship with Jesus Christ, and embracing God as my father, He granted my biological father and I a second chance. I remember it like it was yesterday. After decades of no contact, my mom called me one afternoon and said, "Your father just called me and said he'd like to speak with you. He wants you to give him a call." Instantly, I became infuriated. "He's a coward!" I thought to myself. "Why couldn't he call me?" I realized that my father had been given plenty of chances in the past to become my dad, and he had forfeited them all. No more chances. When I got home, hurt had pushed its way back to the forefront of my heart. "He isn't really my father anyway," I told my wife, "He's just the sperm donor known as my father!" My wife gently kept reminding me of the truth that my father was still my father despite what he had done to me. After a heated debate about whether I should call my father or not, my stubbornness kicked in and I decided not to call him.

Determined to keep my word, I headed to class that night. Then, an uncommon thing happened in the midst of something common. In Bible College, we always opened each class with prayer. This particular night when I walked into class, my instructor immediately turned to the class and said, "I just feel led to pray for the needs of the students tonight. Does anyone have a prayer request?" Students offered their prayer requests one by one. Meanwhile, I wrestled over whether I would be completely transparent and ask for prayer regarding my situation or not. Suddenly, I felt my hand raise. I opened my mouth and out came all of my issues. This truly was a miracle because I am a very private person. Not only did my instructor pray for me, but the entire class began to speak prophetic words over my life! Before I knew it, I was feeling lighter and the huge weight of my burden had somehow gotten lifted in the presence of the Lord. I made up my mind that I was going to adhere to the leading of the Holy Spirit and call my father. I didn't want to hesitate, so during our class break, I called him right then and there; no time to waste. As soon as the phone rang, my father answered. Breaking the silence, the first words he uttered were, "I'm so sorry." My father apologized for neglecting his responsibilities, and for every indiscretion he had committed. In the spirit of forgiveness, we reconciled after 33 years of being apart!

Regardless of how far I was dropped by life's events, I was never broken beyond repair because God's hand—symbolized by the labor nurse's hands at my birth—was always lifting me up. I prophesy over you reading this page at this moment that in the face of all the adversity you have experienced in your life, you will rise again. You are not a bastard! During the Christmas holiday season of 2010, I was faced with the tragic loss of a loved one. My father died suddenly. He was murdered without warning, and with no time to say goodbye. Now, I can only rely on God to bring closure and mend my broken heart. Believe me, I'm not writing this to play the role of a victim; instead, I'm inviting you into my life so that you may examine the victory I've experienced by having a sincere relationship with Christ. Contrary to popular opinion, bad things can still occur during good times or joyful seasons of life. In other words, troubled waters can overflow, and storms can rain in our lives despite a forecast of clear blues skies and sunny conditions. Trust me, it is hard to stand still when you don't know what you're waiting for or what to do. But, God desires to teach us how to stand still, wait, and listen to Him. If you're like me, you need Christ to provide you with the necessary tools to go through every event in life. See, I've been dealt so many bad hands in life, I can hardly count them all. I have swung hazardously on the monkey bars of depression and bungee jumped head first into a failed suicide attempt. I have survived a broken home, collided with divorce head first, and reaped the repercussions of a bitter custody battle that ended with me being the non-custodial parent. I have been fired from a job I hated, laid off from a dream job, and homeless in a city that I grew up in. Believe me, if there was a stat to fail in, I mastered it already. I hope you caught the hidden treasure embedded in the previous sentence. Master failure.

My intent for sharing my story is to cut the time in half for individuals who can't see their success because of the circumstances they find themselves in. Here are three guiding principles that helped me stay suited for success despite the wounds I've encountered.

1. Master Failure

I learned to master failure. As painful as it may have been, I discovered that the failure I encountered was an intricate part of my development process. Mastering failure comes with the ability to endure the highs and lows of any experience. Ride the rollercoaster of failure on the road to success. Fail fast. In other words, learn quickly from your mistakes.

2. Forgive the Failure

Forgive others for bringing failure into your life. You can't afford to exhaust your time in life by holding grudges and fanning the flames of mistakes made by others. Let yourself off the hook. Exonerate yourself for failing and missing the mark. Free yourself from the self-inflicted straight jacket of failure in order to embrace the success waiting on the other side. Freedom and liberation must first start with you letting go.

3. Fail in the Open

When you hide your failure, you hide your legacy. People need to see where you've missed your target or didn't get it right the first time. The truth of the matter is that buried bones still exist. Private failures remain and show up at inopportune

Suited for Success

times. Of course, you can't share your failures with everyone, but failure to share them at all is a travesty.

I want you to know that you can never fail away the success God has prepared for your life. Wounds and body blows may knock you down for a moment, but you will bounce back. You've been suited and divinely tailored for success despite your scars and imperfections. Throughout the course of my life, I discovered that although society labeled me an inner-city bastard child, I couldn't adhere to that label. BASTARD is defined (in the Collins English Dictionary) as a person born of parents not married to each other. Synonyms: illegitimate child, child born out of wedlock, love child, by-blow, natural child. That definition was too small for me. I went on to become an international motivational speaker, I obtained several degrees, and I am currently CEO of a prestigious organization. Just like me, you're a label breaker. Say this with me, "I am not illegitimate! I am not a bastard. I'm suited for success!"

Chapter 9

You're Not Good Enough

George Rice III

"Chief, welcome back! How's it goin'? I hope you had a great summer. I want to let you know that open gym and conditioning starts next week, and I'd like for you to come and work out with the team. Conditioning will be on Mondays and Wednesdays, open gym will be on Tuesdays and Thursdays. What do you say?" Trying to hold my shock, surprise, and sheer enthusiasm in, I said, "Sure, Coach. Thanks! What time does it start?" That conversation alone with the varsity basketball coach was the perfect way to end the first week of my senior year at St. Francis de Sales High School. I couldn't believe it. Coach personally invited me to work out with the team. Immediately, I knew that this year would be legendary!

From that first week in September until late October, I didn't miss a conditioning session or open gym. Tryouts were held during late October or early November. There were approximately 75 to 80 players who tried out to make the team which would have a roster of 14 players. Tryouts lasted for an entire week. By the end of the week, the list of the new varsity basketball team would be posted outside the office of the head coach. After the first day of tryouts, the list dropped to approximately 50. After the second day, the list was cut to 30. After the third day, the list was cut to 20. After the fourth day, the list was down to 16 players and my name along with 15 other players was still on the list. Myself and two of my teammates who played together on the JV Team rounded out the field of 16. Coach hadn't cut the team down to 14 by Friday as he originally planned, so he told everyone on the list to come back to tryouts on the following Monday. On Monday, tryouts happened again, and my two JV teammates were cut from the Varsity Team, which left me among the 14 players. Naturally, I'm thinking that I made the team. We had one more day of tryouts on Tuesday, after which Coach called me into his office and said, "Chief, I want to thank you for trying out and for all your hard work this year so far.

Suited for Success

I think you're a great young man and it's been a pleasure having you around. However, Chief, this year I'm not going to be able to keep you on this team." With a look of hurt, anger, and disgust on my face, I simply asked, "Why not, Coach?" He responded, "Well, you're just not good enough." As I tried to keep my composure, I shook Coach's hand, thanked him, and walked out of the locker room with my bag across my shoulder and my confidence slowly dragging behind me. I didn't bother to shower or put on dry clothes. I walked home, went straight to my room, and cried like a baby. All that played over and over and over in my head was, "You're just not good enough." I was devastated. I knew that I worked hard and I didn't miss a conditioning session or an open gym that he invited me to attend, but still I wasn't good enough. Coach invited me to work out with the team. He never promised that I would make the team. He simply provided an opportunity. Every day is an opportunity to play in a championship game. We are blessed to receive this invitation because it's never promised. We must understand, appreciate, and take advantage of the time given to us, and utilize it as a phenomenal opportunity to get better.

In response to being cut from my high school varsity team, I decided to play in the Catholic

Youth Organization high school league. The team that I played on and the teams we played against consisted of players who were very competitive but maybe not "good enough" to make their high school teams. Some players never even tried out for their high school teams for a variety of reasons, but our league was still very competitive. I took great pride in playing on my team and in that league. During that season, I played with a chip on my shoulder in practice and in games. Our team went to the Final Four in the state tournament and lost to a very good team from Cincinnati, Ohio. I felt very confident about what my teammates and I accomplished. I often wonder where I would be if I had allowed Coach's analysis of my last performance in tryouts to convince me that I wasn't good enough. Honestly, I felt bitter toward Coach for a long time. I wasn't really sure what to say or do in his presence, but I never disrespected him. In fact, Coach enhanced my competitive spirit and rightfully so. I had something to prove to myself. Maybe Coach was right. At the time that I tried out, I wasn't good enough to be a starter. But, was I not good enough to make the team? As I play back the things that happened during my senior year, I smile. If what Coach said was true, then I should've been cut from tryouts much earlier. If what Coach said was true, explain how I became an important member of another team with a winning record that went to the Final Four in the state tournament. If what Coach said was true, explain the countless number of parents and people who went to my high school and other high schools who said, "You should've been on that team, Bruh."

It was difficult going to class with my close friends who were on the Varsity Team. It was even more difficult hearing about funny things that happened in practice, on the bus, or even really hard practices. I felt like I should've been a part of it all. Ironically, I went to every varsity game on the schedule during the regular season and the playoffs. I supported the team and celebrated with them. According to Coach's analysis, I wasn't good enough. In fact, I was greater than his opinion of me. I was greater than my performance during tryouts. My character was greater because I still carried myself well and played with confidence. I continued to make the honor roll and got accepted into my first choice for college. My present wasn't good enough, but my future was greater than what I could have ever envisioned.

In life, everyone has a specific experience that creates a significant shift in their thoughts, feelings, words, and actions. Some simply accept that the lemons they receive can never be made into lemonade, while others go searching for other ingredients and emerge once the lemonade is sweet. These are what I call "crossover moments." Crossover moments are those in which the momentum shifts once we extract the lesson and apply principles to create habits and systems that elevate us to the next level. Being cut my senior year taught me three very important principles: 1) An invitation is not a promise, 2) You're not good enough, you're greater than. Good enough is average, 3) Sometimes God has to break you to balance you.

Once I started coaching, I realized that the impression I would've made on the court playing with my teammates in between the lines for one season would've never matched the lifetime impact I have had on countless players from the sideline. Had I never been cut, I may have never coached at all. In this case, deference made all the difference. Coach showing me deference humbled me, and to this day it serves as a foundation for my coaching passion. So, thank you, Coach, for telling me I wasn't good enough because it led me to my passion and a ministry that has been fulfilling time and time again.

There are times in our lives when we ask for, prepare for, and pursue a goal but we don't achieve it. Upon doing so, we don't realize that losses are blessings. Sometimes, it's not the goal that God wants us to achieve at that moment, it's the growth that He wants us to experience. Losses are His way of getting our attention. That moment with Coach gave me determination and directed me toward my passion. So, thank you, Coach, for teaching me what not to say to athletes who I've had to cut from my teams throughout the years. That moment has allowed me to be more objective, transparent, and respected. The experience of getting cut and being told that I wasn't good enough, along with other wins and losses during my academic, personal, and professional career, has taught me that my duty as a coach, educator, mentor, and parent is to teach principles and strategies that encourage others to adopt behaviors that produce as many wins as possible.

Most people believe that a coach's effectiveness is measured by their ability to prepare their team in the shadows to win when they are in the spotlight. Coaches are regarded for their ability to lead their teams to win more than they lose. I've had my fair share of success and failure as a basketball coach. However, it wasn't until years later that my former players reached out to me via phone or social media and said, "Thank you, Coach. You taught us so much more than basketball." What most people fail to realize is that in all of the years that I've been a coach, I haven't coached basketball at all. After more than 15 years, I'm completely at peace with saying, "I coach character. Basketball just happens to be tagging along for the ride." Basketball and life are games that require action, reaction, and response. Both also require critical thinking that is intentional. Sure, there are some physical elements that are necessary, but teaching players to think and play both games is more than a notion. Often, we go through the motions with no passion, strategy, or regard for the outcome. When we play the game, we can't merely be reactive and expect to win. Instead, we must be proactive, unpredictable, and instinctive as we anticipate what our opponent will do. Therefore, we must break down the defenses in our lives so that we can confidently, consistently, and effectively develop productive habits, a desire for growth, critical thinking skills, and proper execution that leads to a winning tradition.

Life has three notorious defenses: Doubt, Defeat, and Disappointment. If we desire to live the life we envision, we must know how to break down each one of them. Doubt is a lack of confidence; to consider unlikely, to distrust, mistrust, question, and suspect (Merriam-Webster). Often, we don't achieve or surpass our goals because we lose the battle and the war in our minds before we attempt the task at hand. We don't envision ourselves conquering adversity or accomplishing what other people deem impossible. We allow doubt to poke our third eye out and leave us blind. Defeat is overcoming or being overcome in a contest, election, or battle (Dictionary.com). Think back to the first time you ever experienced defeat and to your most recent defeat. Whether it was a game you lost, a test you failed, a performance you bombed or a relationship, I want you to think about how you felt and what you did to get over it. Hopefully, that moment made an impression or an impact on your life. More than likely, the impression made you believe that failure is the worst thing that can happen to you. Hopefully, the impact made you believe that failure is the best thing that can happen to you. Disappointment is defined as being discouraged by the failure of one's hopes or expectations (Merriam-Webster). There's that word expect again. If there's an expectation that is set and not met, then the result is often disappointment. Why? Because when we set out to accomplish goals in our daily lives, we expect to win even when we haven't adequately prepared or performed. The definition of disappointment should read, "discouraged by the failure of one's hopes or expectations after proper preparation for the task."

When I was cut from the team, doubt, defeat, and disappointment came knocking at my door. In fact, they brought suitcases and sleeping bags because they wanted to stay for a while. I doubted my ability to play basketball and excel at a high level based on what coach told me. For a moment, I doubted my ability to do anything at a high level. I was completely defeated. At one point, I felt like I didn't want to play basketball ever again, but I realized that if I quit playing then I would have proven Coach right. I was disappointed because I trusted him and I expected him to keep me on the team. Doubt, defeat, and disappointment will determine where we will go if we don't have a higher expectation of our current selves, our capabilities, and who we want to become. The three defenses expect us to give up because their attack is so relentless. After all, they've prevented millions of people from winning for generations. If we are going to effectively break down doubt, defeat, and disappointment, we must attack them by using our most powerful offense: Decision.

Every waking moment, there's a decision that we consciously or unconsciously make about what we do with our time, talent, tithe, and tongue. The consistency and chemistry of our offense will determine the frequency of our scoring. Yes, we will have doubtful thoughts of our ability and what lies ahead of us. Yes, we will experience defeat even when we expect and prepare to win. Yes, we will be disappointed when we lose. However, it's our response that will help us consistently break down those defenses. We must anticipate the weaknesses, analyze where they are located, then attack accordingly. What we see appears immoveable, but what we believe about our own ability moves obstacles before we even encounter them. It's a combination of critical thinking, talent, and work ethic. There are three defenses and three decisions that our offense can utilize.

1) Decide to Disregard

We must create a system to completely disregard negative thoughts and negative people. I'm sure you're saying, "Coach, what an original concept." When I say disregard them, that means don't label negative thoughts or negative people as such. Label them as misunderstood and misplaced personnel. They are part of what fuels greatness. Believe it or not, negative people, thoughts, comments, and actions do play a part in our success. We disregard by using counter attacks. In the movie *Men of Honor* starring Robert De Niro and Cuba Gooding Jr., there is a scene when they ask Carl Brashear, "Why are you working so hard to become a Navy diver? Brashear's responds, "Because they said I couldn't have it." He took their negative thoughts, words, and actions and used them as fuel. When we decide to disregard, we must tell our story from the gut with passion, accuracy, and detail while capturing every critical aspect that propels us in the direction that we want to go. In essence, we separate fact from fiction in our minds, our hearts, and in our mouths. It's a fact that all weapons formed against us are simply fictional. Disregard their direction and dominance and run your offense.

2) Decide to Design

We have been given free will to be the architect of our game plan. Dare to design a course of action that accentuates your strengths, masks your weaknesses, and brings you success most frequently. Design a system of unconventional habits that take you out of your comfort zone and allow you to achieve unconventional results. HGTV's *Design on a Dime* invites guests who desire to redecorate their houses to be a part of the show. The guests create a budget then tell a design expert their vision for their project. Often, it's a matter of rearranging or eliminating certain things in order to enhance the current space. They use what they already have in their possession, plus a few extra resources, and ultimately maximize the space and prove to the viewers that there is more than meets the eye. When we decide to design our destiny, we must rearrange and eliminate people and things to maximize the vision and simplify the process. Often, we need design experts on our team to help implement the strategy and remodel our path.

3) Decide to Direct

We have a duty to direct our energy, our heads, our hearts, and our hands toward a vision that is bigger than what we can comprehend. But, first, we must direct our energy toward the Creator. Ellen Johnson Sirleaf, former Liberian president said, "If your dreams do not scare you, they are not big enough." Decide to direct, expect, and protect the things in this life that are important to you. When we decide to direct our thoughts and actions, it must be so deliberate, so relentless, so impregnable that people simply move out of the way when they see us coming. Please don't misinterpret this message to mean that I'm asking you to be rude in order to be successful. I'm asking that your direction be an untouchable force that convinces your teammates to raise their level of focus, work ethic, and preparation. You must maintain a level of play that forces your opponents to fear, respect, and ultimately admire your approach. You're not good enough when you decide to break down the defenses by yourself. You're greater when you get help from the right people with the right tools that will help you make decisions by which you can live.

Chapter 10

You're a Winner

Larry Scott Blackmon

"Never letting problems or pain get in the way. You'll soon find out, there will be no doubt, that you're the one on top. Look out!"—Cameo

"From this moment forward, you have to unlearn EVERYTHING you learned before you came to work for me. We do things a little bit different here." U.S. Senator Charles E. Schumer's words were probably the most transformative and influential words I could have ever heard in my life. At that moment, I was introduced to a new way of not only doing business, but a new way of looking at the world that would drive me to success faster than many of my peers. While Senator Schumer was known for his work ethic and driving those who worked for him to certain limits, I had no idea that this transformative moment would mold me into the person I am today.

There was always an expectation of greatness for me. My father (the founder and lead singer of the legendary R&B group, Cameo) worked his way from the streets of Harlem to worldwide success. Everyone knew that I was his son, as I was affectionately called "Little Larry" throughout the neighborhood. Knowing that I was also musically inclined, I was always asked questions like, "When is your album coming out?" or "Can you sing?" The most interesting question was always, "Do you also wear a red cup?" While I thought about wearing a red cup as a Halloween costume, I figured I would leave the singing and codpiece wearing to my father. Children of celebrities grow up carrying a tremendous burden. Often the expectation is that the offspring would grow up to be just as good, if not better than their parents. There are many cases throughout the country's history where celebrity kids suffer emotional or substance abuse issues because of the pressure. While I certainly have my frustrations at times, I can honestly say that not having those issues is successful in and of itself.

Life led me to a career in politics as one of the top African American political operatives in New York State, working for many elected officials, private companies, and ultimately running for New York City Council in Harlem. I'd like to think that I have been somewhat successful and even if that is not the case, that is the story I am going with! At some point, I realized that we are all born with the potential for greatness! We have overcome so much as a people that we are born winners. The question is, when decision-making time approaches, are we prepared to make the right decision or do we let our environment hold us back? What are the excuses that stop us from revving our individual motors? Are we ever willing to unlearn what we think we know and learn things a different way in order to succeed? My father often says, "Observation is a lost art." Are you ready to observe, then take the greatness from within and from others, apply it, overcome your challenges in the face of adversity, and ultimately win?

What I am going to share with you are five tips for overcoming adversity and attaining success that have worked for me. Success is a relative term, but if you apply these tools, I can almost guarantee that you will win.

1. Are You Hungry?

In no way am I referring to food. Ask yourself, "Am I hungry enough to do whatever it takes to succeed?" Are you hungry or do you give up? When that wall is in front of you, do you stare at it or are you prepared to run through it? Do you pass when you are on the one-yard line or do you want the ball? When it's raining and dark outside, are you prepared to get out of bed and go to work? When your back or legs are hurting, do you give in or are you willing to absorb that pain and keep it moving? Are you ready to sacrifice to be successful? Some of the most successful people in the world often went the extra mile to develop their personal brand and achieve greatness. They were the ones practicing their art while the other people played. How many shots did Michael Jordan miss before he started making them? How many times did the Williams sisters practice at a tennis court in Compton, California, that was substandard and surrounded by gang members who on one occasion attacked their father? They were hungry and never stopped. Jerry Rice was at the 49ers facility two days after winning his first Super Bowl championship. Are you willing to go to your office on Sunday afternoon to prepare for the week's work? Are you willing to take the dirty job that provides you with skills you will need down the road? When you go to the store, how do you look? Do you care enough about yourself to dress properly, or do you wear your pajamas and slippers in public knowing that you were just headed to the local bodega? Can you get to work earlier than everyone else and accomplish your goals? The mere fact that you are reading this chapter and getting great information from the other men in this book means that there is some sense of hunger within.

Very few of my friends may remember this, but I worked in the women's clearance section of the Old Navy department store on 18th. Street and 6th. Avenue in Manhattan. I was living with my brother at the time, and he wanted money every month. So, in between campaigns, I did what I had to do to make my ends meet. I would never recommend working in the clearance section, particularly the women's clearance section at Old Navy; but, I was hungry enough to know that I wanted to succeed, and I was going to do whatever it took to get there. I learned valuable lessons—women's sizes, verbal judo, how to perfectly fold a shirt, and most importantly, give the sisters whatever they want.

In all seriousness, are you hungry? When someone tells you no, do you accept that as the final answer or do you try to figure out an out of the box way to accomplish the goal? I learned that valuable lesson from Senator Schumer as well. If you have drive, determination, will, and the fire in your belly, you are well on your way toward success and overcoming adversity.

2. What Is in Your Personal Briefcase?

Whether we realize it or not, each one of us owns a personal briefcase. I know you must be asking, "What is this guy talking about? What does he mean by owning a personal briefcase?" Nine times out of ten, you can look at someone and determine whether they have a great deal of items in their personal briefcase or not. Your personal briefcase includes all of your educational achievements, your occupational achievements, and other items that help boost your personal brand and profile. What some people of color do not understand is that we should constantly work to add items to our briefcase in order to be competitive. We should constantly stay one or two steps ahead of everyone else to earn just less than what we deserve.

The workspace is extremely competitive. If you do not have the educational background that others have in their briefcase, you place yourself at a disadvantage from the start. So, to that end, you need a high school diploma, an undergraduate degree, a degree from a graduate level program, and more just to level the playing field. I went back to school to attain my master's degree. I also received a certificate when I completed an online organizing and leadership course at the John F. Kennedy School of Government at Harvard University. Remember your briefcase needs to have more than educational achievements. My briefcase tells the story that I am creative. I create music, provide entertainment, and serve as a public speaker. I have taught dance, been on television, been quoted in dozens of news articles, and more. Your briefcase could be full of community accomplishments, workplace accomplishments, or anything that tells a story and sets you apart from the rest.

So, my first piece of advice regarding accomplishing your dreams and becoming successful is to find out what is in your personal briefcase. Is your briefcase full? If it isn't full, are you ready to do what is necessary to add the items that will make you competitive when you walk out the door? Keep adding items to your personal briefcase that help you tell your story without having to say a single word.

3. Ignore the Noise

I realize that I have a high tolerance for pain. For three years, I worked for the New York Jets of the National Football League as a senior manager of public affairs. Growing up as a fan, that was my dream job. During that time, the team did well, but our arch rivals were the New England Patriots. Admittedly, my Jets are in for a few seasons of pain as they rebuild. And while I would never give the Patriots credit for anything, I do admit that I follow the advice of their head coach, Bill Belichick. Above the exit door of the New England Patriots facility in Massachusetts is a quote from Coach Belichick that says, "When you leave, ignore the noise." That quote is one that had an immediate impact on my life.

In order to be successful, you must ignore the noise. More often than not, people can offer their unsolicited opinions about you and what your plans, goals, and aspirations should be or should have been. Many people, particularly from the area that you've grown up in, are quick to talk about you because of how they remember you 15 to 20 years ago. You should be strong enough to know that when negativity comes around or when you hear negative and disparaging comments, you must ignore the noise and keep moving. When I ran for office, I went into it knowing that many people would make comments about me, my lifestyle, how I dressed, my private life, and other things that come with running for office. However, I firmly believed that I was the best person for the job, had the best ideas, paid my dues in the community, and was ready to take on anyone who had anything to say. Some of their comments were hurtful, extremely negative, and insensitive; but, most of the comments were positive. With that said, I ignored the noise and ran my race.

I once interviewed someone to be my executive assistant. As she was waiting in the hallway, a work colleague went up to her and said, "I don't know why you're here, he already knows who he's going to hire." This young lady walked into the interview and flashed a smile that I will never forget. Not only did I hire her, but because she ignored the noise while working for me, she received her bachelor's degree and is going back to get her master's. There are people who are in our lives just to be negative, and there are people in our lives that do not have the vision necessary to succeed. There are people who stand on the corner every single day at the same time just to whistle at you when you walk by as you are trying to succeed. Always remember to pursue success relentlessly and ignore the noise.

4. Networking Is Key

I have a question for you. How many business cards have you given out in the last week? How many did you give out today? I have been fortunate to have a very large network. I give out business cards as if I'm giving out candy. One of the books that had the greatest impact on my life was a book by George C. Fraser entitled, *Success Runs in our Race: The Complete Guide to Effective Networking in the Black Community*. I don't recall where I purchased the book, but I do know that I've had that book in my possession for the last 15 years. That book is one that I recommend to everyone because he teaches us the art of effective networking.

I have been fortunate that throughout my career in music and politics, I've never had to go out and search for a job. I have always been referred or recommended by someone who knew when an opportunity was about to present itself. I could not have attained this level of success without the help of some very good people who thought highly of me and my abilities. Who are the people in your life who have positive opinions of you? Do you belong to any organizations? Are you active in your community? Can other people view your work and suggest you for a potential project? Networking is about more than going to great events in the evening and eating fancy wines and cheeses. Networking is about introducing yourself to someone in the most positive light. It's about touching someone emotionally and mentally. It's about leaving an impression so that when an opportunity arises, the person in charge says, "I know someone who would be great for this." Whether we want to realize it or not, we are all one or two people away from knowing each other.

Overcoming adversity and being successful does not happen in a vacuum, it happens because other people have positive opinions of you. Now, let's not be completely naïve as networking can work the other way as well. If you leave a negative impression, your network can certainly hurt you. I have made my share of mistakes with certain people, including some very powerful people in New York. Time heals all wounds, but it's best not to make those mistakes. So, ask yourself if you are networking effectively. When you walk into the room, do people want to know who you are? Networking is an essential part of success.

5. Think Beyond the Now

My father lived in many great places around this country. I could have been with him, but staying in New York and growing up in public housing was an experience I would not have changed for anything in the world. Given that my mother passed when I was 12 years old, for stability, I stayed in the Drew Hamilton Houses with my grandparents. My parents always taught us that there was a larger world out there for us to see. My grandmother, who had a tenth grade education, would say to me, "I don't care where you go to college, as long as you go." Some people did not have that opportunity and did not have others encouraging them to think beyond the now. Many of my friends were caught up in the lifestyle of selling drugs, hustling to make ends meet, doing hard drugs themselves, and not staying in school. When you are struggling to find financing for your project or to get a hot meal on the table, and your child is screaming and you're trying to figure out what's wrong, it's difficult to think beyond that moment.

Dreaming was my way of not being trapped in the here and now. I encourage you to think beyond the present. Try to think a year or two ahead of where you are in this moment. It is an old cliché that we never know what tomorrow may bring. At the same time, it is also true that if you speak it and you continue to speak it, eventually it will come into existence. When pilots are at 35,000 feet, they are not worried about what's happening on the ground, they are worried about keeping a steady course above the clouds. And, they are thinking ahead to their next checkpoint along the route. As you are going through adversity and facing challenges, tell yourself that this only lasts for a minute, but the real joy will come. The investment today will pay off eventually, if you think beyond the now.

In closing, I hope that you can appreciate the advice I have shared. Also, take heed to what the brothers in this book are sharing. Each one of us have overcome the odds, but we are still working to achieve success. Be ready to unlearn some of your anti-productive behavior and go for it. By using the tips I've shared, you will overcome adversity, jump start yourself on the road to success, and ultimately become successful.

Chapter 11

Life Is Good!

Dwayne Booker

I credit my intentional upbringing (orchestrated by my mother and that wonderful place called Brooklyn, New York) for my fight, perseverance, and mindset. I realized at an early age that there was an expectancy for me to be a high achiever in all areas of my life. Mediocrity, quitting, and complaining were never on my list of options. If someone else could get away with it, that was on them and had nothing to do with me. "What am I supposed to do?" was a question I was confronted with throughout my life. Following that voice led me to the place where I can usually say that life is good!

Methods and Strategies for Overcoming

When I was asked to submit my methods for overcoming obstacles and adversities, I began to write down all of the strategies that keep me going, even when this good life tries to test and discourage me. There is not a day that goes by that I don't have to draw on one of these principles. These principles, as I think about it, have been ingrained in me since childhood. To this day, I can still hear my mother saying, "You know better than that." That statement speaks to immaturity, mediocrity, selfishness, rudeness, and anything that does not fit into the category of excellence. I am not talking about being perfect, but I am talking about being and striving for the best, putting your best foot forward, and doing it with all you've got.

If you have not experienced it already, life is going to throw you some tests that will discourage you, if not totally destroy you, if you do not have the tools to deal with them. Whether you know it or not, we are born behind the eight ball (in sin), but we have been given a way out through Jesus. But, that is another lesson in itself. Back to this lesson. If I had to extract my five most important strategies for overcoming obstacles and adversities they would be: 1) Secure, Guard, and Protect Your Mind, 2) Surround Yourself with Positive People

That Will Lift You Up, 3) Know Who You Are, 4) Listen, Listen, Listen, and 5) Give Back.

1) Secure, Guard, and Protect Your Mind

Mind: The element of a person that enables them to be aware of the world and their experiences, to think, and to feel; the faculty of consciousness and thought (Oxford Dictionary).

My most important and powerful weapon is my mind. I use the words weapon and strategies interchangeably in this writing. I have been in a lifelong training academy called focusing to stay in control of my mind. I try to keep my thoughts on upbeat, positive things that will create rather than destroy. I say try because as life happens and things get on my nerves, I have to come back to what I know works and bring my mind back to that place of purity. If you can train yourself to act on intellect (mind) and not emotions (feelings) you will propel your entire life to where you want it to be. Your entire being follows your mind. I don't want to get into the scientific proof here, but just try it and see. Focus on keeping your mind protected. You will have to listen to different music, turn off your favorite television shows, change your location, leave your friends and find new ones, or quit your boyfriend or girlfriend. It may not be easy, but it will be worth it. You will have to practice keeping your mind in the right place; but, keep at it, it will become second nature after a while.

2) Surround Yourself with Positive People That Will Lift You Up

I have personally been around negative, self-centered, narcissistic people and it ain't good. All of that negativity will drain you and leave you useless for the greater things life has to offer. People who want to dominate the entire visit with praises for them and theirs and have minimal to no conversation about anything or anybody else unless it is to slight others or be negative are not worth being in your life. Most, if not all of them, have self-esteem issues that have not been diagnosed or treated, and you are not their counselor. Get rid of them and do it fast. You will be glad that you did. I know people who constantly complain about their associates, friends, and family. I respond, "There are seven billion people in the world, why are you just living, dating, marrying, and hanging out in your familiar neighborhood?" I know that familiarity breeds contempt, so get familiar somewhere else. Somewhere positive, bright, giving, happy, uplifting, true, authentic. You get the point. Brooklyn happens to work for me, but if it doesn't work for you, go somewhere else. Give it some time and you will see that the negative element that wasn't working for you will be a distant memory. And if you happen to look back, you will see that negativity, darkness, untruthfulness, and yes, unhappiness and depression will still be around them. Positive, well-rounded people can spot the opposite in a second. It's like bringing a baby's doosie diaper into a freshly cleaned all white room. You get the picture, and it is not pretty. Positive people will leave you feeling inspired. You will actually start thinking differently, taking care of yourself better, cleaning your house more, and if you continue to hang with them, life will become really good for you.

3) Know Who You Are

Knowing who you are is very important for overcoming obstacles or not getting into uncomfortable positions in the first place. If most people realized that they are unique, special, and created as a one-of-a-kind, priceless, irreplaceable masterpiece, writing this chapter would not be necessary. But, the reality is vastly different. The truth is that we are created as equal but unique. There will never be another me for as long as this world exists. That gives me motivation to put my unique stamp on this world. All of my experiences in life and the way they happened can never be duplicated. Just knowing that makes me want to solidify who I am and not ever want to be you. That is why it is imperative that you know who you are and embrace it to the fullest. I have said consistently that if you have the right tools and put them into place, life will get really good for you. There are so many people who walk in the shadows of others, and sadness comes over me when talking to them. You never really hear who they are. Instead you hear about who they know, who they are connected to, and what someone else has achieved. There is no expectation for their lives, but so much for their idols. You should never shrink when you are around anyone. If you do, fix it. That is a problem, and you must recognize it and work at getting it right. Personally, I don't let people hang around me who don't have expectations for themselves. I, like many others, like admiration but not to the point of being idolized. You should never live or die by your compliments or criticisms; take it all in stride. Knowing or becoming who you are will fix this problem. Knowing who you are takes time, life lessons, tools, and mentoring. When it is all said and done, you should be able to write your own narrative that reads like a success story. The areas that need work get better and the areas that need to be eliminated are gone.

4) Listen, Listen, Listen

I don't care how old, educated, well-traveled, rich, exposed, wise, seasoned, or well-rounded you are, if you hear something that is powerful make sure you listen. It could change your life. All of the knowledge and wisdom is not with one sector of people. Listen because you will hear what is wrong or right. And if you are putting the weapons together, your positive people will help you sift through what should be kept and what should be tossed; but, the lessons will be learned. When I was younger, I would turn certain people off because they didn't present themselves in a way that I thought was presentable. But, as I became more confident in who I was and realized that being more accessible to different people took nothing away from me but in fact made me better, I listened to people outside of my comfort zone. I am glad that I did. Lord, am I glad! I have learned great things from people from all walks of life and those lessons have shaped who I am today.

5) Give Back

One of the most gratifying deeds that you can do in your life, if you ask me, is to give back. Give of your time, knowledge, money, clothes, jewelry, and anything else that will help someone live a more fulfilled life. Giving should start right where you are and to whomever you desire to give to. You don't have to wait until you feel that you have made it in life. You don't have to give in a certain way. Spread the giving around or stick to one way. Find a cause and start today. Most of my dreams are to help others as much as I can through education, regardless of age. I find that older people have dreams just like younger ones do, even more so because they have lived and seen dead-ends.

In the Bible, Philippians 4:8 tells you the things that you should think on for a reason. A clear mind focused on the right things brings peace. Keep people around you that will check you and encourage you with the truth when you are discouraged or ready to make irrational decisions. Know who you really are. Listen and learn lessons from listening. And don't forget to give back. These five strategies are just some of the methods I use to keep me on track. I pray that you use them as part of your arsenal to overcome your issues.

Chapter 12

Statistics

Derrick J. Redmond

The year is 1988, the setting is Lafayette High School. "Derrick, do you want to be a statistic?!" exclaimed Señora Beiser, my high school Spanish teacher, when she happened to see me in the dean's office for a serious incident that I witnessed. I was 16 years old when she asked me that. Over a year later, I dropped out of school. I was becoming the statistic she asked about; the wrong statistic. Her powerful words would permeate my soul, and from time to time I'd hear her voice while in the midst of my dastardly deeds and cad-like behavior. As a high school dropout, I roamed the streets with my delinquent counterparts from school. We would wreak havoc wherever we went. We smoked cigarettes, marijuana, drank all types of alcohol, attempted to steal cars, and even got chased through

Albee Square Mall by the cops for throwing empty 40-ounce bottles at unsuspecting people. All of this took place right under my parent's nose.

You see, my parents divorced when I was about five. I was the youngest of three children at that time. Statistics. After the split, my mother, my two older sisters, and I made an exodus from Bushwick, Brooklyn, all the way down to the backwoods of Dunn, North Carolina, where we lived from 1976 to 1981. I didn't see my father for five years. Upon our return to Brooklyn, I spent time living in Bushwick with my dad who co-owned our three-family apartment building with my uncle (my mother's brother). I would also spend time living in the Crown Heights section of Brooklyn, and later on in the East New York section of Brooklyn with my mother. What a life. Minimal accountability and two places to rest my head. My parents were hard workers, and although they were loving, they rarely made a lot of time for me in my teenage years. Them seldom missing work meant that I had plenty of opportunities to abuse their trust.

I grew up a sports fanatic, playing and watching every sport I could. I excelled in baseball, basketball, and football. As great of an athlete I was, I never took any sport seriously enough to pursue as a career. My wonderful Dad, James Redmond, who was from Savannah, Georgia, tried out for the Pittsburgh Pirates Triple A baseball team but didn't make it. I guess that's where I got my athleticism from. As a kid, I also excelled in drama. I would get the lead role in all of our school plays, but I never took it seriously enough to pursue it any further. My lovely mother, Hattie Barnes, from Marlboro, South Carolina, was a child prodigy who performed on closed circuit TV. I guess that's where I got my acting chops from. So, you see, I came from a good pedigree.

As a teen, I put stock into all of the wrong things in life. Soon, I became bold enough to regulate my dropout zone to the corner of my block, Madison St. and Evergreen Ave. Every day, I would wake up in the late morning, shower, get dressed, and stand on that corner with my other dropout friends until the wee hours of the morning. My father said very little regarding that because he was battling his own demons of alcoholism, and I felt he knew that I was smart enough to eventually get myself together. My mother, who lived across town, had no idea because she and my dad would rarely communicate with each other. Their dysfunctional relationship pretty much worked in my favor. I decided to lie, manipulate my parents, and throw away the balanced and detailed upbringing they, along with my stepfather, Napoleon, gave me. I abused their trust; however, they could've done a tad bit more to redirect me.

My father, a mix of Irish and Native American, never knew his father. He just knew that his name was James McIntosh. So, how was he supposed to know much about fatherhood when he didn't have an example? Statistics. He did a great job, but I found the loopholes in his fatherhood and worked them to my advantage. My daily experience standing on the corner taught me a lot and prepared me for the life that was to come; the life I had no idea about. We'll get to that later. Mind you, this was the 1980s and the crack epidemic took control of New York City. I saw crimes such as: robbery, assault, drug deals, and murders. I'd been shot at and schemed on, and it drove me to secretly carry a .22 caliber handgun every day. Statistics. Across from the corner we hung out on, there was a funeral parlor called Interboro Funeral Services. The owner's name was Manny. Interboro was the neighborhood funeral home, and people were dying to get in there (pun intended). As teens, my friends and I attended so many wakes and funerals that we became numb to death. Countless people succumbed to drug wars, guilty and innocent. And the way I was heading, I was going to become that statistic

Señora Beiser asked me about years earlier. Let's see, I had four drug addict uncles, a functioning alcoholic father, and a beautiful stepmother, Lorraine, who battled her own demons of dope addiction. I saw these people every day, 24 hours a day. These were supposed to be my role models, especially my father and uncles. Since my childhood role models were occupied with their demons, my teenage role models became sports figures and musicians. The likes of Rickey Henderson, Karl Malone, Kareem Abdul-Jabbar, Prince, James Brown, KRS One, and Big Daddy Kane were the main people I looked up to. However, I had one person in my corner who never judged and always encouraged me, my older sister, Moniece (aka Niecy). She would take time to make sure I didn't lose my mind because of my surroundings. She called me periodically just to see if I was okay and to redirect me in life. I lovingly refer to her as my second mother because since childhood she went that extra mile to protect me and our oldest sister, Adore.

After wallowing in the mire of the streets for almost two years, I once again heard Señora Beiser's voice loud and clear in my mind. So, I decided to enroll in an alternative day school and night school. To prepare myself for school every morning and evening, I played a song written by

Slick Rick in 1988 called, "Hey Young World." That song was very pivotal in my transformation. I was on my way.

Did the Bell Ring Yet?

"Rick, my company didn't come," she quietly told me. I was 19 years old, armed with a high school diploma, and no job. Malissa, my gorgeous 17-year-old girlfriend was pregnant with our first child, Davon. Statistics. Malissa and I had known each other since we were mere toddlers; our families literally grew up together. She was from the East New York section of Brooklyn, where she lived with her mother and three siblings. Her parents, like mine, were no longer together. Malissa's upbringing was very similar to mine, but vastly different. Some of her uncles had also succumbed to drugs. Here we were two teenagers from broken homes, with no money, not a pot to wash in, and one high school diploma between the both of us.

Malissa was "churched." Thanks to her mother, she was raised in the church since birth and knew the Bible from front to back. I was the opposite. My sisters and I sporadically went to church with my dad before and after the divorce. On July 29, 1988, before the pregnancy, I fell in love with Malissa as I watched her dance to "Set it Off" (a rap song by Big Daddy Kane). I knew from that moment that she was the one. Years later, we became teen parents. Statistics. On October 21, 1991, at 9:50 p.m., our son, Davon Jay Redmond, arrived. My life as a delinquent was over, but I had no job. Enter Derrick Wright, my older cousin through marriage. Derrick was from the Bronx. He was an Army reserve who was cool and boisterous, but very respectful. He was married to my cousin, Barbara, and since both of our names were Derrick, we automatically clicked and became close. Derrick always called me Slick, a term of endearment because it rhymed with Rick, which was short for Derrick. Cousin Derrick would drive me throughout the five boroughs of New York City in search of a job, any job. Being a father is something that I wholeheartedly embraced, and I couldn't wait to provide like a real man does. I found a job in Queens, New York, as a shoe salesman and stock clerk at a women's shoe store. It was only a 15-minute walk from my father's house in Brooklyn. My salary was $4.00 per hour. Yes, you read correctly, four. And I only worked 20 hours a week, so you do the math.

No longer did I grace the corner with my presence, I now had a son whose birth saved my life. Every day after work, I would go to Malissa's mother's house to take care of Davon while Malissa went to night school to attain her high school diploma. Once she came home, I would leave between 11:00 p.m. and 12:00 midnight. Mind you, Malissa lived in the projects, Boulevard Houses to be exact. Unbeknownst to her, I stayed strapped with my .22. Thank God nothing ever happened to me. Besides dealing with idle threats behind my back from a dude in her projects who got jumped in Bushwick by my friends, street beef never seemed to come my way. Regardless, no one was going to keep me from seeing my son, no one. Even if I had to discreetly murder him. Statistic.

It's Raining Rice

"I do," Malissa and I both confessed at church in front of family and friends. Reverend Desha Moten, the pastor of the church Malissa grew up in, Rugged Cross Baptist Church, pronounced us husband and wife. We were married on May 21, 1994. We now have two children, our son, Davon, and our one-year-old daughter, D'Asia. I'm now working in Greenwich Village at a high-end furniture store, and we live in our own apartment on the same Bushwick block where I spent most of my life. I was a proud family man who could still hear Señora Beiser in the distance. Statistics.

Suited for Success

I was on top of the world! However, everything came crashing down on June 27, 1995, the day my hero who lived two houses down from us died. That night at 9:00 p.m., my 8-year-old brother, Tyleek (the child of my father and stepmother, Lorraine), was outside playing. I was befuddled and questioned him as to why he was still outside playing at such a time. He told me that his dad went somewhere. I knew right then what was up. The Lord had prepared me for such moments. My father was only 51 years old; however, he was sick from heart disease due to years of drinking, bad eating habits, and insurmountable stress from the divorce. Statistics.

My dad could not leave the house without assistance because his feet were too swollen, so I prepared for the worst. I climbed through the backyard window because there was no answer at his door when I knocked. I entered and quietly called out, "Dad? Dad, where are you?" No answer. As I began to walk around the apartment, I finally saw him sprawled out near the kitchen floor, seemingly lifeless. I began nudging him to wake up because I recalled sometimes finding him in the same exact position, in a stupor, as a teen. This time he did not awaken. Imagine the hurt a son feels when he finds his father dead. It's a hurt that never fully dissipates. My precious, nurturing, loving dad was gone. Honestly, he was the only one who said, "I love you" to me as a kid. Up until eighth grade, I would kiss my dad on the cheek before going to school. Now, here I am 22 years old, married with two children, one on the way, and no clear direction.

But, Pastor Said

On New Year's Day of 2003, I rededicated my life to Christ at our church, Christian Cultural Center (aka C.C.C.), led by Pastor A.R. Bernard, my new role model. At this point, Minister Malissa (yes, she's now a minister), is one of the praise and worship leaders at C.C.C. and is travelling the world ministering through song. She had the voice of an angel since childhood, and combined with understanding of the Word, Malissa became a powerful child of God. I was teaching kindergarten at a day care center, and we now had four children—Davon: 19, D'Asia: 17, our daughter Dhane: 15, and our two-year-old daughter, Dallas. Once again, I was on top of the world! However, on January 31, 2010, Malissa was in a car accident that required spine surgery and left her voiceless. I thought, "No, Lord, not my baby! Why?" I was devastated watching my wife suffer. Privately, I agonized and wished that we could switch bodies; but, the Lord would remind me of what Pastor Bernard once said, " Crisis reveals character." I knew it was time to keep a brave face and step up my manhood.

As time went on, we began to struggle a little bit financially. Things got worse when my job had cutbacks. I now only worked half a day. One day out of the blue after service, the Lord sent Dr. Laurie Midgette, the children's ministry director and the principal of Culture Arts Academy Charter School, to offer me a job as the dean of students. I excitingly accepted. Even better news, my wife slowly worked her way back into form and became a certified New York State Chaplain. Inspired by her, six months later, I became one too.

Won't He Do it!

We were back on track! I was the dean of students, my wife was ministering again on Sundays, our older daughters were in college, my son was employed, and little Dallas was a student at my school. I enrolled in an online school to attain my master's in education in order to further the ministry God was obviously setting me up for. In June 2015, I was chosen to be an honorary member of the International Christian Brotherhood fraternity by my dear friends, Director Dr. Onorio Chaparro, and his second in command, Rodney Patterson. They were two men who helped to change my life years prior. I guess they felt I had something to offer. They saw the God in me. That same year, I was invited to preach at a church. It was my first time publicly ministering. Whoa! I wasn't afraid though. I just wanted to represent Pastor Bernard correctly because the burdens of being under a global pastor of a mega-church can be nerve wracking for most. However, pastor quickly put that to rest by redirecting my attention to representing God. He told me that God trusts me, and furthermore, he said that he trusted me. "Be yourself, Minster Derrick" were the last words he uttered in our 15-minute meeting. That was the same advice Dr. Chaparro gave after closing our meeting.

The message I taught was centered around the importance of manhood in Christ. Due to a long planned ICB event at C.C.C., there were only about 15 people at my sermon; but, I taught like we were in a 20,000-seat arena. In attendance were my wife, my mom, Dallas, and a few close friends. But more importantly, my son was there. He got to see his father come full circle, from a teenage father with no direction to a man of Christ-likeness standing up there and teaching God's Word. Wait, the story gets deeper. Remember the Interboro Funeral Services across the street from the corner where my friends and I hung out? Well, ironically, I was the officiant of three homegoing services there. One of the services I officiated was for one of the close friends I grew up with who stood on that same corner with me. Another was an older brother of one of my corner friends. And the last one was the father of my close friend, who also stood on that corner. Prior to that, at a church in that same neighborhood, I assisted my wife in officiating a homegoing service for the son of one of my closest corner friends. Imagine going back years later to the very same spot where death began, only to be born again and serve as a shining example of what God can do. Realize though that this story isn't about me, it's about the path God has chosen for me. Believe me when I tell you that the journey is nowhere near completion. And it was all inspired by one heartfelt question from my angel, Señora Beiser.

Final Answer

As her question remains, I now have an answer. "No, Señora Beiser. No quiero esa estadistica." I want to be the right statistic, the creator of my own statistics. The statistics of redemption. The statistics where they said no, but God said yes. The statistics of being obedient, trusting, and having faith. I am the proud owner of these statistics, they're mine. Gracias, Señora Beiser, for I owe part of my life to you. As I close this chapter, remember this Scripture, "Don't let anyone look down on you because you are young, but set an example for the believers in speech, in conduct, in love, in faith and in purity (1 Timothy 4:12, NIV). Amen and amen. Shalom.

Chapter 13

Catalytic Leadership

Paul Coty

History is a great teacher and there is no substitute for it. History has taught me that there's a special place reserved for the first in anything—the first manned flight, the first man to walk on the moon, the first African American U.S. president. I too come from a family of firsts—my grandmother was the first registered black nurse in the state of Iowa, her daughter (my mother) was the first human resources director in Cedar Rapids history, and her son (my brother) was the first African American CEO and president of Horizon Human Services. I've recently experienced my own first—becoming the first African American vice president of Young Life in New York City. Young Life is a global youth ministry reaching nearly 1.7 million kids annually in more than 90 countries. I have the privilege of overseeing Young Life's mission in New York City, operating local ministries in 19 of the 59 community-districts across the five boroughs that serve more than 10,000 youth. In 2003, I joined Young Life NYC's regional staff as director when there were only four members on the team. By 2006, that team would dwindle down to an inauspicious three—me, myself, and I. When others try to account for how we were able to make the leap from the humble beginnings of a $200,000.00 budget to a $3.5 million operation to date (representing the most dramatic expansion in the organization's 70-year history), I reflect on my own history and how it served to shape my approach to faith, leadership, and service.

I am the oldest of six children, but the only child of Paul H. Coty Jr. and Harriet Robinson. They were married and divorced by the time I was four. I remember tearful goodbyes as a child when leaving my dad after one of his scheduled weekend visits. He was my hero. And to my mother's credit, she made sure it stayed that way. Still, the older I got, the lonelier I became as I watched other sons enjoy what I could not—their father's presence. Although I didn't fully appreciate it at the time, I did have a prayerful and conscientious mother who devoted herself to me like no other. She had a wonderful gift for two things: teaching the Bible and hospitality. Our house was always a welcome respite filled with guests from all walks of life. We always had over relatives, neighbors, her girlfriends, or members from our church. During my early years, our family attended a Baptist church; but, when I turned 11, we became members of a non-denominational ministry named Gospel Tabernacle. It was there that my mother's hospitality changed my life. When we officially joined the church, I was fortunate that it was a ministry which attracted and was attended by a rare combination of men. They're makeup ranged from your average business professional to your typical college student. And every so often, these men from our church would visit our house at the same time. As in any town and on any main street in America, churchgoers predetermine a preferred destination to congregate following the traditional Sunday service. That go-to-spot was our address in Cedar Rapids, Iowa. This was because Harriet was celebrated widely for the way she got down in the kitchen. As a byproduct of her fame, having interesting men with whom I could form significant relationships with began at those meals and would forever change my life. The men around that table helped me navigate the toughest moments of my adolescence and remain fixtures in my life today.

Their presence was what I desperately needed in the absence of my father. As one of four black students in a graduating class of 465 in Northern Iowa, I was growing up and learning how to become a man surrounded by other young men who didn't look like, talk like, or live like me. I spent much of adolescent life angry and disappointed. I continued to be disillusioned by relationships which placed my skin color above my character and capability. It would be disingenuous to suggest that I didn't have white friends to whom I was very close. In fact, I had plenty of friends who were white, but I had to work hard to relate to them completely. They lived in and saw the world very differently than I did. And, they often had access to a very different group of people and resources than were in my network. It's within this struggle that my mentors began to intervene, helping me to order my steps in what was an uncharted world. They taught me the value of shaking a hand, giving a smile, or being friendly in order to make friends (as the Bible teaches).

Keith Chappelle was one such mentor from my church. Throughout high school and most of my college career, I would be Luke Skywalker to his

Master Yoda. Keith happened to be a national sales director for PFS (Primerica Financial Services). He allowed me to travel with him to national conferences and sit in on several sales training sessions. Oftentimes on our travels home, he would debrief me about what I had learned. He was trying to determine if I had picked up any strategies on how to interact and engage people that would eventually translate into my own style. Growing up in the cradle of Iowa where less than 10 percent of the total population are people of color, Kevin's tutelage meant a great deal to how I would develop as an organizational leader. The greatest gift one could give anyone is the gift of access. Keith gave me that access to grow and develop as a professional.

Fast forward to September 2, 2003, when I joined Young Life's staff in Hell's Kitchen, NYC. I had been reined into the ministry by two close friends, Christine Garde and Troy Grant. When I arrived, we formed a small team charged with growing local youth ministries in the world's largest and most challenging market. Our greatest concern was that we were accomplishing great things in ministry that few people knew about. In 2006, the winds of change would come quickly and change the course of Young Life in the city and my career with the organization. The year prior, our small team would break apart and I can honestly say I had a hand in its unraveling. In the earliest stages of building our local mission, my biggest stumbling block was the relationship I had with my supervisor—we were oil and water—two guys who were pursuing the same goal but could never agree on an approach. If one's methods determine their approach and approach determines success or failure, we were on a collision course for absolute collapse and disaster. The tug of war was long, and the battle was intense. My biggest chores were developing the ability to speak truth to power and navigating both the noticeable and unknown tensions of race. Early on, there were several theories I had to challenge (i.e., kids of color are responsible for theft. In actuality, the majority of theft is an inside job). I recall correcting statements about the capacity of men of color to be adult guests because of a lack of financial resources. I even confronted statements and jokes that were racially insensitive. My prevailing thought was, "If I don't address this, every staff person of color that comes behind me will have to endure the things I was too fearful to address."

The enmity between my supervisor and I was most likely attributed to my many years of playing and coaching basketball. I've always been driven by competition and enthused by adversity. I have developed resolve under pressure and have been passionate about helping people work as a team. But perhaps what I most loved about the game is its finality; at the end there can only be one winner. Admittedly, I viewed much of my professional journey up to that fateful moment in 2005 as a competition. For me, there had to be an adversary and a hero. Thankfully, one day I woke up and discovered I was playing the wrong game. In my head, I was playing basketball when I should have been playing golf. Golf forces you to play against the field. It's you and the course. If you play the course well, where and how you finish is a byproduct of your internal work and preparation rather than the contention between competitors. It's a game of clarity and focus which requires you to slow down, be in the moment, forget the last shot, and prepare for the next hole—all valuable life lessons. There would be several more to which I can attribute my success as a leader.

#1: Stay the Course

That one decision eventually altered my career. Instead of leaving the mission due to an epic struggle of wills, I decided to stay. Instead of quitting, I continued to play. Like Nehemiah, I kept my post on the wall, deciding to remain until the vision was complete. Realizing then that the primary goal was not to "beat my boss," I instead began to focus on all that was being asked of me from above. The Lord had given me a clear picture of what I should do and where I should go, and my job was to remain focused on that goal. I was to run my own race, finish my own course, and not pay any attention to the small handful of people I perceived were determined to stand in my way.

A few years later, at a Christmas party in 2009, I ran into one of the gentlemen who brought me to Young Life in 2006. He appeared incredibly surprised to see me—almost too surprised. He said to me, "So good to see you. But, I can't believe you're still here!" I simply responded that I had never entertained leaving. No matter if the leadership changed (which it did), or my team left (which they did), or my position changed (which it did), building Young Life in New York City was the assignment to which I had been called. I had a daunting task in front of me, but I wasn't going to turn back now.

#2: Survey the Field

Surveying the field helped me identify the individuals who would be vital to the mission's success. Surveying the field meant connecting the right people to the right opportunity. The selection process was important, and I understood that I needed to put the right people in the right places. In exercising this principle, I would find people in non-traditional settings. We eventually recruited and pulled in candidates from a variety of sectors, including but not limited to: education, business, entertainment, the arts, communications, and finance. As I surveyed the field, here's what I knew would be required of me—love Christ and love kids. I knew the Lord would teach me the rest.

#3: Become a Great Storyteller

Young Life was a suburban phenomenon that captured the hearts and minds of parents and kids within communities of means; it was not a known entity in New York City. On more than one occasion people I met would say, "Yeah, I've heard of Young Life. Don't you sell life insurance?" My task was to build a brand and appeal to a donor base that would recognize our need for financial support to transform the lives of kids in the city. Every day we were building positive relationships with young men and women across the city and no one knew it. We learned the hard way that the power of a good story should never be underestimated.

A good storyteller knows that in order to be successful in their delivery, their words must be as vivid as a painting or as moving as a symphony. Too often, people forget the power of their story and the importance of the journey they have lived. A clear example of this is in ministry. There is an evident gap between ministry impact and the public's impression of what actually takes place in ministry. The only effective way to bridge the gap between the important work ministries carry out every day and the obscure ideas people sometimes form about ministry work is through the power of sharing our story. This revelation at once sparked something inside of me. My brain exploded with so many thoughts about what it takes for full-time ministry workers to become better storytellers. For inspiration, I looked no further than Jesus, who we know was a master storyteller. His stories were compelling, challenging, poignant, and easy to repeat. When ministry members begin to communicate their stories in that way, they connect people intimately to what they are experiencing every day in the field. This ultimately unlocks their imaginations, allowing the story to become a truly powerful tool for attracting support from stakeholders over the long-term. This brings us to the driving principles of great storytelling. To be effective, you must actively include the following combination of ingredients: Vision and Preparation, Placement and Formation, Frequency and Inclusion.

#4: Speak Truth to Power

The Scriptures tell us to be shrewd as a serpent but harmless as a dove. When speaking truth to power, there is a way to address both without burning the house down. Scripture also says that the Spirit will teach you what to say and how to say it when you are placed in front of folks in positions of leadership. Often, our approach to a conversation determines our success or failure. I had to adjust my approach by downplaying my passion so that my message could be heard. Removing "the angry black man" from the room helped my presentation.

Speaking truth to power also required that I increase my capacity to hear and ask good questions. When I was promoted to regional director, my boss, John Wagner, gave me a book called *Power Questions*. I became better at asking powerful questions so that I could have insightful and powerful conversations.

#5: Have a Vision and Be Prepared

Vision determines your method of impact. Make sure your vision is clear and write the vision down to make it plain so that those who read it may run with you. During preparation, sit down and think about what you want to communicate regarding your vision. It takes time to identify the point of your story, and to capture in words the picture that comes to mind about your ministry's impact. Early on, I dedicated several hours to clarifying my thinking and direction. The more time I spent with the vision, the clearer I became and the easier it became to articulate it. During a meeting in 2010, I stood before a group of leaders and said, "My prayer is that the Lord never moves me until the picture He painted for me is clear to the city and to the world."

10 years, $3.2 million, 45 staff members, 450 volunteers, and 10,000 kids later, we're still going strong!

Chapter 14

Rising Above Feelings of Rejection
Steven Carter

People don't reject you, they only reject the responsibility that comes with being connected to you.

You are probably thinking, "What can this brother from Brooklyn tell me about rising above rejection with all of his education and what seems to be a successful life?" I know that is what I would ask myself. However, I want to share with you that many of my achievements in life have, unfortunately, been born out of insecurities and feelings of rejection. I learned at the tender age of thirteen that I was adopted. I was left at a hospital as a premature baby with five surgeries in the first six months of my life, and the doctors told people not to adopt me because I would not live to be one. Even with this blessed reality, I still struggled with feelings of rejection. I felt rejected by my biological parents for abandoning me, a sick child due to no fault of my own, and rejected by my loving parents who adopted me but kept that reality hidden. This untimely revelation, by my aunt who accidently released the breaking news to me, sent my life into a whirlwind. I began looking for affirmation and validation in all the wrong places, the wrong people, and through many destructive habits. Have you ever felt unloved, unwanted, abandoned, insignificant, hurt, lonely, and so many other negative feelings that arise when one feels rejected? If so, keep on reading. If not, do me a favor and keep on reading.

There are many forms of rejection that one can experience. Although mine revolved around being adopted, you might feel rejected for reasons such as: job termination, romantic relationship or marriage failure, friendship betrayal, family disappointment, or self-defeat. Sometimes, we might even feel rejected by the One we want to believe is a loving God. That's right, the pastor said it! Sometimes life itself can make you feel rejected by God. However, I want you to know that regardless of your condition, you too can rise above those feelings and accomplish whatever you set your head and heart to do. In the following paragraphs, I will share with you four principles that have helped me overcome feelings of rejection and empowered me to continue moving toward greater successes. But, before I share those practices, let me add that you will never reach a state of perfection where those feelings will not arise again. However, when they do arise, you will know how to keep pursuing your goals and dreams. Are you ready? Are you sure you are ready? Ok, let's get to work my brother.

#1: I Can Rise Above Feelings of Rejection by ACCEPTING Myself

I don't care who you are, you are responsible for your life. I say in my book, "You are not responsible for how you arrive in this world, but you are responsible for what you do while you are here." Sometimes, the easiest and most practiced method of survival is placing blame on parents, family members, communities, friendships, relationships, and sometimes even our churches. The reason why I know this is true is because this was what I did for a very long time, 36 years to be exact. I blamed my family for my actions that caused me to live beneath my potential. I used to say things like, "I will never let someone get close to me because they may abandon me like my biological parents did." Or I would say, "The reason why I act a certain way is because I have to. I know everyone is out to get me." In other words, I was not comfortable with me. So instead of examining myself internally, I placed blame externally. Little did I know, I was not hindering anyone but myself. If I wanted to be better, I had to totally accept myself with all my flaws.

In order for you to reach your greatest potential, you cannot be afraid to look at yourself for who you are—the good, the bad, and the ugly. Once you begin to look at yourself and you are honest with yourself, you will be able to grow into the dreams you have for yourself. Guess what I did? At the recommendation of a mentor, I enrolled in therapy. Me! A pastor! Someone who is supposed to encourage others. In therapy? Although it was a tough decision that challenged my pride, I am thankful that I did it. I was able to learn that, as I say in my book, "Therapy is not a sign that you are crazy, but it is a sign that you love yourself enough to keep from going crazy." We all need both spiritual and professional help. I don't know where you are in your personal development journey, but even if therapy is not for you or you do not feel totally comfortable with the idea, I recommend that you find a trusted friend who can be honest with you about your strengths and weaknesses. No matter how tough it may be to hear some of their comments, listen clearly without any pushback. Like me, you may be surprised that a lot of what you are facing has more to do with self-sabotaging habits than with external circumstances.

Three Flaws I Need to Learn to Accept About Myself and Improve

1._____

2._____

3._____

#2: I Can Rise Above Feelings of Rejection by ADVANCING Myself

You remember what I said in the previous point about not placing blame on others? Well, the same is true for your personal development. No one else is responsible for making you a better you. You have to decide to read books, attend seminars, listen to YouTube videos, enroll in school, seek mentors, and explore other avenues of self-improvement. One of the best ways to advance yourself is to always hang around others who have already succeeded in whatever you are trying to accomplish. For example, as a pastor who desires to continue to build a thriving ministry that impacts the lives of thousands of people, I hang around and learn from other pastors who have already accomplished what I am dreaming to become. Let me give you a secret that has worked for me and I believe it is universal. When you are hanging around others who have achieved the success you are pursuing, never act as if you are already on their level. Always remain in the role of a student, and they will happily pour their life lessons into you. Trust me on that. For example, if you are recently released from prison and you know you do not want to go back, find someone who was released from prison and has succeeded. Ask them to help guide you. If you desire to be an attorney, find someone who is already a successful attorney and seek to learn as much as you can from them. If you make excuses for not advancing and improving yourself, you will never be able to reach your dreams. Whatever you desire to do can be accomplished if you are willing to do the work that is necessary. That's a fact. Don't allow anyone to tell you otherwise. The bottom line question is, how badly do you really want what you desire?

What Are Three Ways I Will Advance Myself?

1. I Will _____

2. I Will _____

3. I Will _____

Who Are Three People I Know Who Can Help Me Advance Myself?

1. Name:_____

Telephone: _____

2. Name:_____

Telephone: _____

3. Name:_____

Telephone: _____

Action Step: Contact the three people you listed above and let them know what you are trying to accomplish. Ask them if they can be of help to you or recommend someone or a service. Now, don't call if you are not serious because one thing successful people don't waste is TIME.

#3: I Can Rise Above Feelings of Rejection by DISASSOCIATING Myself

In order for you to truly become your greatest and reach your full potential, you are going to have to cut negative things and people out of your life. One prayer I always encourage the members of Mount Ararat Baptist Church (MABCBK) to pray is very simple yet very powerful. It goes like this, "Lord, please remove whoever or whatever is in my life that You did not place there, and please place whoever or whatever in my life that You desire." This is very important because we are the sum total of the five people we hang around the most. Likeminded people hang together. Therefore, you have to examine your family and socials circles and ask yourself: who are the people who are adding to you and who are those who are taking from you? Now, allow me to keep it real. There are some people who don't mean any harm, they just don't know any better. However, if you are not careful, they can project their limitations and fears onto you and cause you to doubt your possibilities.

Suited for Success

Once I decided that success was in my future, I had to make tough decisions and release or pull back from people who only offered me words of discouragement instead of support. Allow me to give examples of the habits of some of the people you may need to eliminate from your life or at least pull back from. They are people who are: content with failure or mediocrity, always criticizing others, negatively communicative about life, always complaining, constantly reminding you of your past, always partying and never producing, always involving you in bad experiences, blind to your potential, jealous of your achievements, insecure with themselves. If you are not careful, regardless of how much you love them or how long you have been friends with them, they can kill your bright future. The reason is because it is easier for them to pull you down than for you to pull them up. You can never want success for someone more than they want it for themselves. If you continue to hang around passionless people, they will rob you of all the energy you need to achieve your goals.

Who Are Some People I Need to Pull Back from OCCASIONALLY or TOTALLY?

1. Name:_____

Why: _____

2. Name:_____

Why: _____

3. Name:_____

Why: _____

Action Step: Now, don't call them and say, "I am not hanging with you anymore." Just decide in your head and heart that you will not be as accessible to them. If they ask you what's up, simply tell them that you are focused on what you are trying to do and don't have as much time as you had before. You never know, that may inspire them to become productive. If not, you will know that you made the right decision. Never apologize or feel guilty for making decisions that will improve your life.

#4: I Can Rise Above Feelings of Rejection by ANOINTING Myself

Hey, don't get mad or uptight. I am a pastor. I had to put something "preachy" inside of this message. However, what I am saying is true to my faith. Pray over yourself and let God know about your struggles and how you really feel. Don't think you have to be super religious or know the Bible from front to back to pray. All you have to do is be sincere in your prayer to God. When I am praying to God, I speak directly to Him because He already knows my struggles. Here are some practical prayers you can say over yourself. "Lord, I want to be a business owner, but I don't know how. Please connect me with the right people to show me how to accomplish my dreams." "Lord, I want to be a better father or husband, but I have not had a real role model and I don't know where to start. Please send male examples into my life who can help me become better in this area." "Lord, I was just released from prison and it is hard to get a job. Please lead me to the right people and the right places to help get my life on the right track."

All I am saying is that you have to talk directly to God if you want to have the fruitful life you desire. Allow me to warn you though. When you pray, be ready for what God will say to you. Let me give you a heads up! His instructions will usually not be your preference. But, if you obey them, they will lead to your purpose. For example, the last place I wanted to be was Brooklyn, New York. I was just loving the life of the South—low cost of living, affordable homes, nice weather, etc. However, God led me back to Brooklyn, and I came fighting. Thirteen years later, I now see that this was where my purpose was; but, I would have missed it had I not prayed and followed His guidance. I am writing this because brother Kearsey in Brooklyn (who I would not have met had I not obeyed God) asked me to. I don't know what you are trying to do, but it is possible regardless of what people say or think.

The Word of God says in Philippians 4:6 (ESV), "Do not be anxious about anything, but in everything by prayer and supplication with thanksgiving let your requests be made known to God." This simply means that there is nothing you cannot ask God to do in your life. Your only assignment is to pray (make the request), work hard, and leave the rest to Him.

What Are Three Things I Want God to Do in My Life?

1. I need You to_____

2. I need You to_____

3. I need You to_____

Congratulations, Brother! You are on your way to accomplishing your goals. Apply these principles to your life and don't allow anything to keep you from moving forward. I leave you with these words… some rejections are blessings from your Creator in order to set you up for opportunities you would have missed. You can rise above your feelings of rejection or you can allow your rejection experiences to keep you where you are. The decision is YOURS! May your life continue to be filled with success. I pray and hope that my story will open your eyes to the greater purpose for which you were created.

Chapter 15

Secrets to Employment Success
Craig Palma

Employment doesn't take skill, employment takes strategy.

In 2002, I was recognized as volunteer of the year by Junior Achievement for outstanding service to young people. My driving force is to help young people and adults understand the different aspects of employment. Employment is like an engine. It can work even if a part is missing, but it won't work well; and, if enough parts are missing, it won't work at all. After seeing how difficult it was for young people to find work and being motivated by the shock of a sudden lay-off of myself and hundreds of dedicated Verizon managers in 2006 (which was tantamount to corporate downsizing), I decided to take my knowledge and future into my own hands. Today, I put the power in the job seekers hands by providing my book, *The 10 Step Pocket Employment Guide*, which covers every aspect of employment.

I was born into poverty in Harlem—a section of New York's inner-city fraught with urban-societal issues, mainly drugs. I was raised by my grandmother due to my father being a drug dealer and my mother being a drug abuser. As a young man, I had anger issues and was placed in foster care. I learned how to deal with my anger by reading comic books. I have had 40 jobs in my lifetime. Some people would say that's a bad thing, but it's actually a plus because it allows me to impart my experience in a way that helps students. Some of the organizations I've worked for are: Verizon, AT&T, Sprint, Errand Solutions, the East New York Youth Alliance, the Police Athletic League, Junior Achievement, Macy's, FEGS, STRIVE, Goodwill of Greater New York, and Fedcap. While working for some of those organizations, I've counseled and trained hundreds on employment and attaining career success. As an employment strategist and career coach, my coaching style is based on the belief that career transformation cannot be sustained without life transformation. If you want to be happy, it is important to understand your strengths, weaknesses, and the direction you ultimately want to pursue. My honest and direct approach is motivational in nature, but more importantly, informative. Helping individuals find their career purpose is my goal. Many people never find their dream job; but, if I can help individuals transform their lives so that they are happy with their chosen field, then they will never work a day in their life.

We are never taught every aspect of employment; therefore, most people will struggle and languish. I had to figure it out too. I'm often requested to speak with and train clients in Corporate America and the nonprofit community, but the most satisfying talks I give are to students in middle and high school because I'm able to give them insight that they can't get from a textbook. I've been told I have a charismatic, dynamic, and uniquely engaging style to my presentation. My genius lies in my ability to reveal the truth and teach the secrets of obtaining employment in this new era. I'm completely honest with my participants. I don't pull punches. My "Success Essentials" workshop has helped young people and adults understand the different skills and techniques requisite for gaining employment. I also provide some insight into the insider hiring secrets, to teach people how to master any interview for any job in any industry regardless of your qualifications, education, or experience.

In school, you are expected to have certain core requirements. In life and in the employment world, those same core requirements are expected as well. It is imperative that people understand how to establish a plan of action, why education is important, and how to select a career for long-term success. The first step is the acquisition and application of the core skills needed for long-term success in life and business. The reality is, people are never taught how to get a job or attain lifelong career success. At the heart of employment success lies certain core values such as: Brainstorming, Evaluating, Decision-making, Innovation, Researching, Planning, Leadership, Productivity, Social Skills, Flexibility, Active Listening, Navigating information, Organizing, Social Media navigation, Communication, Identifying goals, Application, Development, Creating, Revision, Using technology, Description, Explanation, Analyzing situations, Flexibility, Initiative, and Speaking. I'll briefly go over some of the major aspects of employment so that you can be great!

Goal-setting introduces fundamental techniques starting with establishing short-term and long-term goals. We must first gain a consensus as to what those goals should be. If you don't establish a deadline for obtaining employment, then you may find yourself embroiled in a fruitless drive (in some cases for months, and in many cases much longer). In addition, through goal-setting, you will learn to anticipate and plan for problems.

Assessment is designed to enhance an understanding of basic, practical applications. My "Success Essentials" course focuses on real-life processes such as: self-evaluation and determining a career path when things seem next to impossible, or at least improbable. In some cases, you have to simply take a look at the world around you. I used to think accomplishing certain things was impossible until I realized one simple fact—if someone else is doing it, I can too. Planning for employment success cannot be achieved without an effective knowledge of how employment works. Most states have some form of free job training. Take advantage it. Knowledge is power! Research at libraries, browse websites, and check with schools. When you get a job, learn as much as you possibly can and make yourself invaluable to the organization. When hired, you will receive the training you need in the first year or two, and you will have a chance to learn new things. The type of training varies with each job. Take advantage of it.

Knowing what to say to employers, understanding the job market's peaks and valleys, and identifying who's hiring is important for employment success. In addition, developing a winning two-minute pitch, constructing a winning resume, identifying what an employer is looking for, and knowing how to take advantage of opportunities is paramount to securing gainful employment. My course features over 50 different careers to examine, ranging from simple calculations and graphs to full-featured experiments with solutions.

First impressions establish the foundation for all future interactions. There is never a second chance for a first impression. So, I designed my course to help students become more aware of themselves as unique individuals. Using their own experiences as a guide, students are encouraged to be cautious of how they use social media. They are also given lessons on how to construct a lasting brand, how to dress professionally, business etiquette on the internet, and proper ethics that should always be followed no matter how informal an interview may be. Networking is the most powerful tool a person can have because of the importance of communication. It also helps for developing lasting relationships.

Job searching can be a difficult task. Most people use what I like to call a static approach to employment, but the fastest way to get employed is to use a systematic approach. A static approach involves applying for a job in a passive manner. For example, applying as people tell us about employment opportunities. The problem with this approach is that we have to play the waiting game when it comes to employment. My approach, the systematic approach, involves creating a list of employers you want to work for which allows you to become more proactive in your employment search.

Resumes are a snapshot of your life, and people tend to use a one size fits all approach when it comes to them. Most people don't realize there are different types of resumes, and a well-drafted resume always catches the employer's eye. Resume writing lessons help students to draft their own resume based on the latest trends in the business world. Resume writing teaches students how to tailor their resumes as their education advances and work experience grows. They also learn how to construct a Federal resume and use key words.

I have specific dialog I use when training individuals to seek employment because you must know what to say to decision makers when you speak to them. Interviewing should be the easy part of the job search process, but it can often be the most difficult because people tend to talk about certain aspects of their personalities as opposed to painting a picture for the employer by using certain terms. My training helps to develop basic skills and creative thinking, and students are asked to explore their vocabulary and how they can convince an employer to hire them.

The most difficult aspect of getting a job is successfully convincing an employer that you are the best candidate. To do that, a prospective employee must be able to answer some tough interview questions. You should know that there are some standard questions that everyone should be able to answer, and there are questions that will surprise you and throw you for a loop. I want you to be prepared for whatever you are about to face and get your top dollar.

Employment says you have convinced the employer that you are the best candidate for the job. I try to get people to understand the traditional theory regarding obtaining employment while also providing instruction and modern theories on how to maintain employment and progress. The subject is taught at an introductory level for new employees in the workforce, but also helps people who are established as well, allowing the average student to grasp the concepts and complete their mission of obtaining employment. It is important to both maintain employment and progress during your time at a job. It is also important to decide what the next step is. Have you taken this job as a place-setter until you obtain another opportunity? Do you see this job as long-term? Will this job help your career objective? Establishing a backup plan and a good relationship with your employer is critical to your success.

Chapter 16

The "Facts" of My Life

Xavier Porter

"It takes a certain type of man to teach. To be far from hood but to understand the streets."—Drake

My life story began on May 30, 1977. I was born addicted to drugs, to a drug-addicted woman who (through the grace of God) was unable to care for me. As a young man, I was told many times by many people that I wouldn't amount to be anything in life. I was told often that I would either be dead or in jail by the age of 18. But, here I am! I have survived so much pain and agony in my life and I hope, pray, and believe that whoever is reading this can survive and make it through too.

My life story consists of selling and using drugs, having a lack of belief in myself, and becoming homeless. Like others, I've been traumatized from losing friends and family throughout the years. While experiencing unfortunate situations, I came to find my purpose in life. I found that there are people in this world who need constant and active support from others; so, I discovered my passion to help others change their lives for the better. I've worked in the fields of mental health, substance abuse, and human services for well over 20 years. From working in these fields, I have gained more empathy for and insight into humanity, which are important qualities needed to get through life. But, that's not all that's needed to get through life. As an African American, you also need an education. Education is the key to success. I was once a young man who feared school. I entered college at a young age and became sidetracked with what was taking place around me. I eventually dropped out. As I continued to entertain the negativity around me, I began to dream that something was missing. I became broke and homeless. I was sleeping in bathrooms and at times a friend's home or in a car. I awoke and said, "Is this going to be my life?" With time and support from people who truly cared about my well-being, I was able to recover and focus on what mattered to me the most: my family.

After being discharged from the Navy for a positive urine test due to marijuana, I entered Job

Corps. I had nowhere to go but up. I completed two trades—certified nursing assistant and certified child care nanny. I returned home, found employment, and never looked back. However, obstacles still found a way to enter my life. I lost my job, bounced around from position to position, and then found myself working for an organization where I realized I would be a great asset for helping people change their lives. Since then, I became a father, graduated from college with a master's degree in public administration and affairs, and networked and established genuine relationships while also developing my own website where I cover the sport of boxing. I've interviewed many boxers including: Floyd Mayweather, Bernard Hopkins, Oscar De La Hoya, and Roy Jones Jr. (my all-time favorite fighter). It is here where I found my passion and felt that my purpose was truly warranted and needed.

This book is filled with many great men who have achieved success in their personal lives. But, what does success mean to you? Does it mean being wealthy? Rich? Popular? How does one become successful and maximize it to its full potential? We all have different goals and dreams. I can only speak from experience and encourage you to find your purpose in life and fulfill your dreams. You will come across naysayers and people who will try to distract you from achieving success; but, you mustn't let anyone or anything come between you and your destiny.

My role in life is to inspire others. I believe that is my destiny. I believe God has put me here on Earth to be more of a supporter. I've experienced great things in life, from being adopted by loving parents and raised in a loving and nurturing household to having my own loving family and great career. My hope and prayer are that my story and life experiences will help the next person achieve their dreams and goals.

"… as I grow yearly. I can see things more clearly, that's why they fear me!"—Nas ("Hero")

Chapter 17

The Path to Success

Troy Harrison

First Thing's First

A black man in America living past the age of 40 is an accomplishment in and of itself. I often reflect on how Malcolm, Martin, and Medgar died so that I can continue to live and be a man of success. These prominent men of the Civil Rights Movement gained success by advocating for the rights of people of African descent and minorities. Speaking and preaching for the voiceless, they gave their lives in order for other black men, like me, to be successful in a society where it appears the odds are against us. So many of us are the products of their fight; a fight which still continues.

Natural Born Leader

I am the oldest of three boys raised in a single parent household. I am the oldest of 17 grandchildren. Since childhood, I have always gone the path less traveled. I did things my way, the different way; yet, I led the pack. I've been the first, and always the first to make a difference. From pledging on the founding line of the Pennsylvania Beta Kappa Chapter of Iota Phi Theta Fraternity (a nationwide historically African American collegiate fraternity) to moving to New Jersey from Brooklyn and using my newly minted Kinapps Natural Hair Care Salon skills to open the first natural hair salon in the state of New Jersey, it was about being the first.

As a captain in the fire department—a career path not often afforded to someone from a disenfranchised African American community—I've chosen to blaze a path less traveled as I serve my fellow man by being willing to sacrifice my life to save the lives of others. My walk through many less traveled paths is, in a sense, a protest against the mainstream. The transition and process in each achievement was never easy, never routine. I had the confidence, but I also had to do the hard work and put in the time that average will never strive for. In my salon, working six to seven days per week and 12 to 14 hours per day was my norm. That

Suited for Success

was a must in the early years of building a natural hair care brand and leading a lifestyle change in a new community. Studying and training were necessary to become a firefighter and to move through the ranks. These periods of hard work, hardship, diligence, and delayed gratification are the periods that so many of our youth don't see. They only see the accomplishments of success. But, there's no sugar coating the road to reaching success. You've got to put the work in and be willing to stay the course. One may said that I'm a no joke, bad ass brother. To that I would say, "Thank you."

I think back to going toe-to-toe with that Pottstown country dude while in college, then suddenly feeling a vibrating blow to my face that caused me to black out and wake up on a stretcher in an ambulance. I was all bloody with a deviated septum from a pipe being smashed into my face. There I laid in General Reading Hospital waiting for the plastic surgeon specialist. He was talking about giving me a Michael Jackson nose. I said, "Nah, just repair the one I came in here with." The newspapers said, "In Philly, an 18-year-old Kutztown University student named Troy Harrison from Brooklyn, New York, starts riot in the middle of the campus." All I was really trying to do was defend myself and retaliate against cats that jumped one of my boys in the cemetery near the campus. Well, downing a fifth of Southern Comfort that day probably didn't help me in decision-making. However, getting hit with that pipe might have been the turnaround in my life because even though I was in college it just seemed like I had no direction. But, after that incident, I turned my first semester 1.9 grade point average into a 3.8. I even tried to be a one woman man for a little while.

The following year, I took a serious look at myself. I felt somewhat lost, confused, and all alone; so, I did some hard soul searching and sought out what some call knowledge of self. College had not been my first choice. The Marines is where I had an interest; however, graduating from high school at 17 meant that I needed consent from my mom. But, she refused saying, "No son of mine will be in that white man's Army if I have anything to do with it." So, as the scholarship offers came in, I decided to try the college route to become a great architectural engineer.

My mom, a strong, black single parent did the best she could to raise three snotty nosed boys. Mom was my first real live, concrete role model of success, working her way off welfare and earning a bachelor's degree in education from Brooklyn College. Mom instilled in her boys that education was a priority in life. I tell people that I was going to college as early as seven years old because when Mom could not get a babysitter for us, she drug us to school with her, sat us in the back of the class, and dared us to make a sound. Since Mom was an education major, if a class topic was about children, we would be used as props for the discussion in the lesson. Mom made sure that we had positive mentors by having us join Troop 375 of the neighborhood Boy Scouts, and she kept us in and out of the Boys & Girls Club. Mom was very careful about what men were present and who she brought into the household. Raising her boys was her world. Keeping me off the mean crack-infested streets of Brooklyn was her priority. Thank you, Mom.

That second year at Kutztown, I skated through classes while partying in all the New York clubs (from Bentley's to Latin Quarters), bar hopping in Reading, Pa., bootlegging Sisco (some say it's like drinking liquid crack) from New York to Pa. to make a few dollars, and being the center of the college social party life. Despite my popularity, it seemed like I was in some kind of culture shock because where I grew up, whites were few and far between; but, on campus and in the town, whites were the predominant population and I felt uneasy around them. There was a disconnect. By spring semester, I found the connection with Greek life by pledging a predominantly black fraternity (actually, the only black fraternity I could see myself pledging at the time), Iota Phi Theta. Their colors were brown and gold, and the red, black, and green in the shield really intrigued me. It also intrigued me that this was the first line in Pennsylvania of this national fraternity. To this day, I Phi till I die.

Back and Forth to New York

That summer, I still felt like I didn't belong and was alone in Kutztown. It seemed like something was missing. So, before I wasted any more money and time, I decided to check out the real world by staying home in N.Y. and getting a job. Reading books like *The Isis Papers* by Dr. Frances Cress Welsing, *Countering the Conspiracy to Destroy Black Boys* by Jawanza Kunjufu, and Dr. Haki R. Madhubuti's *Black Men: Obsolete, Single, Dangerous?* opened my eyes, and I began seeing my life and the world a whole lot different. Yes, pro black is what I was now striving for. I realized I was lacking knowledge of self and was striving for an identity. Reading a book about Booker T. Washington helped me to find my direction in working with my hands and landing a great vocation and career path as a barber.

And, not just any ordinary barber. I was both a client and a model for Kinapps Natural Hair Care Salon, internationally known as a pioneer salon for natural hair care. Through my experience with the salon and my own exploration of self-development, I started to feel a sense of fulfillment in my life that college did not give me.

Desiring more sense of self and knowledge of caring for natural hair, I decided to take an apprentice course at Kinapps. From the beginning of the apprenticeship, I found serenity and joy in this new experience. Within a short period, my natural talents were evident, and I knew that following this new passion would change my life and the lives of many that I would have the opportunity to connect with through the natural hair care industry. In servicing clients at Kinapps, I noticed that a number of clients traveled from New Jersey to Brooklyn. By being in tune with clients' needs and through my own research, I quickly realized that the opportunity of a lifetime in natural hair care awaited me just across the Hudson River. Cutting, twisting locks (dreads), and braiding hair like never seen before was a part of the cultural boom in the community. So, I branched out across the water to New Jersey to start the first natural hair care salon of its kind. I called it Afrakuts, which stood for Africans for revolution actively keeping umoja through style. It felt really good to see clients lifted after sharp, short haircuts or freshly done twists. I knew that I would help to give people (and myself) a sense of confidence to go tackle whatever they needed to do in the real world. Sometimes I spent five to six days, eight to 12 hours a day making a difference in the community. I met all kinds of interesting folks from drug dealers to judges, derelicts, and musicians. Police and black firefighters (something I never saw growing up in the streets of Brooklyn) patronized the shop. You name it. Anyone and everyone came to the shop.

Nowadays, children in the community get to express more creative hairstyles—fades with parts and designs, flats, slopes, twist looks, and braids. Society has embraced people of color wearing hairstyles that represent them instead of trying to look like others. The wave of being happy and nappy started to be more than just a trend; it is a way of life. But, growing up, barbershops gave basic haircuts—low, close Caesar cuts, fades, and shaped afros.

Looking to Do Something That May Not Be the Norm

I jumped at the opportunity to become a firefighter. Something about helping the community intrigued me. After learning about the schedule and seeing how it wouldn't conflict with the business, I tried my hand at it. As one of the oldest in the academy, I may have appeared to be a hindrance; however, there was a certain kind of respect and relationship I acquired with my classmates due to my maturity. Now, as a captain in the fire department, the proud dad of a son who is also a Newark firefighter, and a mentor to many others, this path has been very rewarding. At times, it might seem a little hard to juggle these hats; however, serving the community and my fellow man while knowing that it is God's will and my calling gives me the strength to do it day in and day out.

Life may lead you down many roads. I seem to choose the roads less traveled. More and more people in my world are traveling down this road with me. Ultimately, I've chosen the right direction—serving my fellow man and uplifting others. "Each of you should use whatever gift you have received to serve others, as faithful stewards of God's grace in its various forms" (1 Peter 4:10, NIV). Doing something that is needed, making a change, and doing well in the world are the ultimate signs of success to me. As I strive to raise my four children to live conscious and intentional lives, I realize that without adversity, pressure, push back, negative experience, hardship, loss or life-altering experiences, neither success nor growth can happen. I firmly believe that one cannot fully appreciate success or internalize the journey to success if one's experience is solely that of being a high achiever or always having desires met at their beck and call. When there has been no struggle or sacrifice, the achievement of success may be taken for granted. My darling offspring seemed to be oblivious to real world struggles in the context of their own lives, until the misfortune of not having a cell phone for 24 hours became their reality. Yes. Really. The world was coming to an end because not having the world at their fingertips made the struggle real.

I believe that Buddha's 10 Rules of Success best summarize the life I have strived to live. According to Buddha, you should: find your own path, become undaunted, take small steps toward your goal, work hard, think positively, embrace your failures, not compare yourself to others, get the right friends, live a balanced life, and remember that your travel in life is about the journey, not the destination. I believe that although the path of success ultimately is a subjective experience, there will be common ground along the journey. Every person will have to sacrifice wants, build character, learn from mistakes, lose and build relationships, fail in little and big ways, and ultimately find a sense of accomplishment on their own terms. Choose your path.

Hopefully, I have made the rugged paths smoother for those generations who will come behind me. I invite the unborn to stand on the shoulders of my uncommon choices. I challenge them to chart new uncommon paths, and to spread wider paths for future generations of brothers and sisters from our community. As I reflect on the cusp of turning 50, I am happy, and I feel blessed. I'm a happily married man to my loving and gorgeous black woman who is strong and supportive of me. Together, we have raised one man-child into adulthood and continue to mold his three siblings. To me, the riches of a successful life outweigh any amount of material riches. I have achieved uncommon success as a captain in the Newark Fire Department, a pioneer and entrepreneur in the natural hair care industry, and as a black man. Damn! I guess I can say that's success. However, none of this would have been possible without my spiritual drive to serve my community. Whether it be in the shop bringing people's crowns to their glory or fighting fires for life safety, incident stabilization, and property conservation, I will continue to strive to be a great husband and the best father I can be until the sun sets on my life's journey. When my name is written in the Book of Life, I hope that what will be noted is my compassion for people, and my desire to be a positive role model for brothers and sisters in the community who may not have a traditional education or life path but want to define and find success on their own terms. I hope that people will remember my ability to connect with others, from the infant to the elder, and inspire them. I hope that someone will write that I was unashamed about my love for the Creator and my family. I hope to be remembered as one who did not always follow the well-beaten path, but who created my own unique paths and found success and fulfillment in doing so.

Chapter 18

RISE! From Thought to Fruition
David Marquis

What drives and motivates a person? Is it a desire to prove that they are driven no matter what? Or could it be the personal need to pay a debt to society? Whatever your reason, one must choose to make forward progression in life. I've thought about these questions in personal reflection for some time now. It is my hope that my personal experiences will motivate you as many in my life have motivated me.

Let me share with you my first glimpse of motivation growing up. It was right there in my own home while watching my mother. She is still a strong pillar in my life today. I would watch her go on the subway from the South Bronx to Brooklyn. This took a minimum of 10 hours a day, six days a week. At this time, I was just a small child who really couldn't comprehend the sacrifices she made as a single parent. My dad passed away and she was left alone to raise two young boys in the South Bronx, Kelly Street to be exact, in the 60s. Let me paint the picture for it wasn't always a pretty one. We saw gangs and drug addicts daily. Not exactly motivation for setting goals in my life. Now, wait, this isn't written for sympathy or as a sob story, but as motivation to never quit! For she could've, but chose not to cower in sorrow. My mom pushed me and my brother. She had us reading at higher grade levels. She set the bar high for us which afforded us the opportunity of being bused to more affluent schools. This was a choice that I'm grateful for to this day.

While attending school, we met all sorts of people of various shades and colors that I wasn't used to being around. One would tend to have an inferiority complex in these situations, especially growing up where I did. And guess what? That was me. I have never been around that many Caucasians in my life. Did I give up? Stop going? No, I didn't. I chose to turn the situation into a positive one and I pushed myself to excel in my studies. I tried to work the hardest and be the very best. When it came to my appearance, I made sure to always be on point. I dressed to the tee every day. As a young man in grade school, I was excited about picking out nice

Suited for Success

shoes and suits to wear. My mom would try to deter me from dressing up, but I wanted no parts of that. Dressing up made me feel good about myself. Greatness is our only option. Do you comprehend what that means? To be destined for greatness? To be destined for greatness means that no matter what you will be great. Let that thought sink in. This task, at times, can't be accomplished alone. Whether it's parents, a friend, or an educator, these key people can help you survive and get through this life. Their help can make you strive to do more, be more, and help others more. Here are two questions for you to ponder: Who is that driving force for you? What are you trying to accomplish in life?

I asked myself those two questions throughout junior high school. That is the time one may start coming into their own as a person. As you embark on this stage in life, you'll find out who's who, what's what, and how to take responsibility for your own life. My lessons during this time took place at Castle Hill 127 in the Bronx. At that time, it was a mixture of students. Various avenues of trouble were right at my fingertips. Luckily, someone took an interest in me and veered me into playing basketball. Basketball taught me to be well-rounded which assisted me in my young adult life. Playing on a team also taught me confidence when speaking to others. Have you ever felt nervous to get involved in a conversation based on lack of knowledge of the subject matter? Well, you're not alone. I too used to feel that way. However, I learned very quickly that you have to have a voice in order to be heard. This voice aided me as I earned a college scholarship to Texas State University where I played ball with some elite people who made it to the NBA. Being a leader also gave me great confidence. Stop and think for a moment about what can give you confidence? Is it playing on a team? Being a part of some social club? Or can you be a leader at work? To make it in today's world, it's up to you to: 1- Have a voice and 2- Display confidence. Having multiple avenues to gain confidence also aids in the journey. I've walked many paths and I'm grateful for all the opportunities.

Take a walk with me down memory lane as I discuss a few of them. I dabbled a bit with doing work as an electrician. I found that this profession didn't satisfy my adventurous side; so, I decided to join the military as an engineer. But, guess what? My earlier training came into play. I was enlisted as an electrical engineer. This didn't make me exempt from combat however; so, the man who wanted adventure, repelled out of helicopters and jumped out of airplanes. This races my heart to this day. But, I won't stop there. I was shipped to Alaska. That's when things turned around some. Alaska was a totally new life for me. I had to get used to the darkness, the cold temperatures, the five in the morning formations, running ten miles daily, no women, no drinking, suffering from cabin fever, and working 14 hours seven days a week. Many times, I thought, "Man, forget this. I want to quit." But, there's no such thing as quitting, no calling in sick, no "I don't feel like doing this today," and there's no coming in late. You have to be disciplined.

We've all heard that phrase, "There is a light at the end of the tunnel." Right? At times we may lament and think, "Yeah, right. Where?" But, don't give in to doubt. That light is there even though it will be dim at times. Refocus and work through those roadblocks. I did it while being in the military. And, regardless of what you are presently going through, you can do it too. I'm not writing this chapter to be preachy. I want to drive you to do better in life. Let's fast forward out of my seven years in Alaska. I'm back in New York now, and fully aware of the things and life I'm leaving behind. I'm back in the thick of things, and moving with the movers and shakers. Music was always my outlet and I landed an internship position working with music and concert promotions. For two years, I had the honor of meeting some key industry people as I got my feet wet and learned the ins and outs of the music business. Those times were often very challenging because I've found that it's not what you know but who you know that gets your foot in the door. Yet, giving up was and never will be a part of my genetics. Those noes eventually led me to start my own little record label, along with providing A&R assistance for some major labels. That venture kept me quite busy for over 20 years.

My belief is that one should be able to evolve and be willing to learn new things so that just in case one door closes, you can survive by going in another direction. This new direction taken was a fearsome one at first since I never in my life thought I would be able to breakthrough. I'm speaking of the cologne, perfume, and apparel business. Whether it's picking fragrance samples, designing the cologne bottle, picking out the fabric for the garments, or meeting with the design team to make your vision come alive, one comes to find a true accomplishment when it's from the fruit of your own labor. Have you ever thought of being an entrepreneur? What is preventing you from doing so? Are you afraid of failure? One must make a choice and leap! There will be a net or perhaps you will fail. But, try again. I've heard many noes in life, but in my mind the noes weren't really noes, they were not right now's.

Pressing forward on yet another avenue in my life, I embarked on working for an influential real estate firm on the East Side of Manhattan as a personal chauffeur for the family. In this position, I have had the pleasure of meeting so many diverse people. Working closely with the partners, I get to see and pick up on the business savviness while having jewels of knowledge dropped upon me to help me fine tune my own business endeavors. I take to heart the fact that they aren't too busy to listen to me, and the support thus far has been tremendous. I'm grateful to be a part of this team of moguls, yet I'm not stopping at admiring them. I too strive to be the very best and set a fine example. I strive to not become too busy or self-absorbed, but to remain a willing vessel of servitude in society and for my wonderful family.

Earlier, I spoke about my mother being my rock; however, so many others in my family drive me to be the best man I can be. In particular, my grandson. He's been influential from the first day he was born. He is such a bright young man in the making. I've taken him under my wing to show him various aspects of my life. He's coming into his own now as he embarks on middle school. My grandson is being guided by a solid family structure (which is very important now and for the years to come). By keeping up with his studies, he is soaring to the top of his class. I share this part of my life as an example that you never know how you will impact someone's life. If you don't presently have someone to take under your wing, perhaps become a mentor or a big brother or sister to those without siblings who are looking for positive role models. You'd be surprised to find that a listening ear or a shoulder to lean on goes a long way.

Sharing the various experiences of my life has been my pleasure. It is my hope that I was able to motivate you. I'm no expert, but I am a man who is striving to be the very best no matter what curve balls have been tossed my way. To press ahead, one must have a spirit of not quitting. In addition to my spirit, I've had many solid people in my life. I pray in my years to come to have new solid people, as I'm just touching the surface. We all need to be driven, and it's key to have people in your life who are just as driven as you are, if not more. Don't settle for just getting by in life or being mediocre. That's not what we were created to be. Until this pad meets this pen again, stay blessed and focused my people.

Chapter 19

Till Faith No Longer Possesses Parameters

Norman Grayson

Every living male (whether aware of it or not), has gone through, is going through, or will go through that defining "MAN UP" moment. When I say Man Up, I do not mean in terms of how the hood may prescribe to handle a situation because given the wrong kind of influence or attention, it could result in poor decision-making and have severe penalties, consequences, and repercussions. I mean Man Up in the sense that you decide to go against the odds that have smothered your road to success and strategically make adjustments for a better future. As the chameleon relies on camouflage as a means of survival, learns to adapt, and adjusts to its surroundings, so must the black man living in America. With the odds being stacked against you and black men becoming more recognized as a statistic than a brand in the making, the last thing you want to do is subscribe to the propaganda of the media and stack the deck against yourself. The fact of the matter is, there is a serious problem that exists in most homes where there resides a black male, young or old. As my loved and respected late Bishop Clarence V. Keaton used to say, "What do you do when you don't know what to do, when something has to be done?"

Are you feeling left behind or out of the loop? Are you uncertain about the direction your life is headed in? Is your life headed in any direction at all? Not only have I been there, I took residence there. And let me share with you that until I decided to go against that thought of despair, provoke and implement a spirit of commitment to be better, and cease listening to destructive criticism nothing would have changed. Nothing happens without making a commitment, not even faith. The Bible says, "Faith by itself, if it does not have works, is dead" (James 2:17, NKJV). Works is another way of implying commitment. I use it as a reminder of what I can do when my spirit is in alignment with my purpose. I want to share with you that every new challenge you face will come with its own set of obstacles tailor made just for you. But, if you have a vision or goal and mix it with integrity, establish a level of knowledge, combine that with consistency, and navigate the course, not only can you decrease or even eliminate the stress of the emotional rollercoaster, but you can turn any tragedy into transportation. No matter what happens to you, how you choose to overcome it is what can bring the most gratification as you cross the finish line of your trials!

My Man Up moment came to me in the summer of 2000. It's understood that when you wake up in the morning, have your breakfast, kiss your family, and walk out of the front door, it could very well be your last day to see the sun. A known cliché that has become common yet taken for granted is, "Tomorrow is not promised." Well, by God's grace I have been blessed to see over 17,484 days of tomorrows that were not promised to me; so, in hindsight, it should not have come as a surprise when my faith was tried. Let me back up a bit before I share what happened. Growing up in the East New York section of Brooklyn, from the sports that we played in the streets to the games and activities in the public-school system, I always considered myself the athletic type. We used to play sports from "Can't see in the morning, till can't see at night." By the time I reached college in 1990, my knees and body were so worn down from all of the basketball played on the concrete that it forced me to take a long hiatus from the activities. I was not about to allow the doctors to convince me that cutting my knees open then stitching them back up would make them better. Instead, I ended up joining a local church, True Worship Church to be exact, and gave my life to the service of the Lord and His people. By the mid-90s, within the span of three years, I married my then girlfriend of six years, had my first child, was hired by the telephone company, opened my t-shirt printing business, and earned responsibilities in the ministry. But, as my family, job, business, and ministry responsibilities expanded, so did my waistline! From 1987 to 1994, I gained 42 pounds and went up eight sizes from 34 to 42. There was no longer a "pro" in the active and no "extra" in curricular activities. I was leaning on the arms of Gawwwwwd. All 232 pounds of me. Church responsibilities eventually became every day of the week, along with late night binging of hero sandwiches, and food from the local bodegas and the Lindenwood Diner (I still eat there to this day). You know, the strange thing about church is that if you're not paying attention you can end up becoming so busy being busy that you miss the point of being effective. While in the midst of servitude, you can actually lose your way and end up serving selfish needs and becoming a victim of your own devices.

Now, back to my Man Up moment in the summer of 2000. One night, while on my way to a choir event, I noticed that there was something not quite right with me. Not with what I was wearing (because I was pretty fly as a fat guy), but in my body. The way that I felt, the way that I was acting, and the way that I moved were all very different from my normal self. I shared it with my wife and we agreed that I should make a walk-in visit at the local medical center. I remember having some blood work done and waiting in the room. The doctor, a tall plain-looking gentleman with an unreadable posture, walked in with a tan folder in his hand that contained one sheet of paper. He said, "I have some good news and I have some bad news. Which would you like first?" Naturally I said, "The bad news. Let's get it over with." He responded, "Well, the bad news is that you are now a diabetic. You can live, or you can die. The choice is yours." I found myself bathing in the sweet noise of silence, which sounds like the perfect place when your mind is at peace. But, when in the company of bad news, there's turbulence and confusion equivalent to gridlock on a Friday in the middle of NYC at 6:00 p.m. when the president is in town and there's just one lane that's allowing you to merge into the Lincoln Tunnel. On one hand, I could have become angry about the doctor's lack of sensitivity, but there is no real way to share bad news, because in the end it's still bad news! His bedside manner left a lot to be desired (at least he could have made an attempt to deliver this news in a comforting way); but in retrospect, he was open, honest, and kept it 100. There was no telling how many times he gave out that same speech to others, maybe under even worse conditions. To him, it was physician's business as usual. Then, he went on to say, "If you choose not to take care of yourself, life could be very difficult and severely painful. But, if you make healthier choices and incorporate a better lifestyle, you could live a healthy, normal, and productive life."

I remembered his words as I re-enacted the encounter later that evening. But, at that present moment, all I could hear ringing in my ear was, "YOU'RE A DIABETIC, DIABETIC, DIABETIC, DIABETIC!" Me? The athlete? A diabetic? How could this have happened? What is this sorcery? "God, how could YOU have let this happen to me?" I asked. You know you have gone off the deep end when you begin to blame God for the repercussions of your actions. After all, consequence is no coincidence. Luckily, God winked at my temper tantrum and so-called adult behavior. I was walking in circles, dumbfounded by what had just occurred, and trying to wrap my head around this new lifestyle that the doctor was talking about. This lifestyle that is supposed to be absent of banana pudding, barbequed everything, and all flavored soda... SODA! I looked side-eyed at everything I was involved in as if they were the culprits, when all I had to do was check the reflection in the mirror. What troubled me the most was that I knew better and got caught out there. I come from a family with a history of Diabetes Mellitus (the proper term), which is derived from the Greek word diabetes meaning siphon (to pass through) and the Latin word mellitus meaning honeyed or sweet. This is because in diabetes excess sugar is found in blood as well as urine. It was known in the 17th century as "The Pissing Evil" ("History of Diabetes" by Dr. Ananya Mandal, MD. www.news-medical.net), and boy was I pissin... and pissin... and pissin... and drinking crazy amounts of water only to start the pissing game all over again! You see, on my father's side of the family, it was introduced to me as diabetes. But, on my mother's side of the family (the southern side), I had "sugar." So, I walked around calling it sugar diabetes until I understood better. I wondered how in the world I was able to get both.

This is where the confusion really began. On one hand, I was very overweight for a 5'8", 31- year-old African American who had just been diagnosed with a condition that the doctor said could lead to a normal happy and healthy life by doing the right thing; yet, I was surrounded by people who were diabetics, with lifestyles that did not reflect what my doctor had stated. They were experiencing major complications from heart disease and high blood pressure to amputations and eventually death. So, my hope was shot and pretty much on its last leg (pardon the pun). Not to mention that by that time I had lost my dad, whose voice I could still hear from the grave saying, "Boy, I told you this would happen." My life, my marriage, my business, my job, and my faith all began to spiral downward as if the plug was pulled in the tub. As it drained, I was struggling to grab ahold of the water.

Did I reach you yet? Am I touching your situation? There's an old country saying I would hear my siblings say when I was younger that goes, "Can't kill nothing and nothing won't die." That pretty much means that you feel as if nothing you put your hands to is working in your favor and you should give up all hope. By this time, I had added another 39 pounds to my frame and tipped the scale at 269 pounds. I remember that alone feeling like I had hit rock bottom. But, even when you're at rock bottom, it also means that your feet are planted on something solid that you can use to regain balance, strength, and control! One night while in prayer, I recall asking God for the umpteenth time, "Why me?" I think that God got tired of the pity party coming from my mouth, so He replied, "Why you? Why you? Child, why not you? How will people confirm and testify about what I have placed inside of them, unless their comfort zone is removed? If I select you, then I can erect you." He said some other really cool stuff as well, but the point He was making to me, which is the point I want to make to you, is that the things that should have made you bitter are designed to make you better! You are a winner, you were born a winner because from the beginning you won the race for life over millions that were just like you. But, you were the one that fertilized your mother's egg first! You may feel like a failure, but the only way that failure can have a success story is if you refuse to quit! It's true that failure is not an option, it's actually part of the process. Giving up is not an option either! Stop looking for the secret to success. The secret to success is that THERE IS NO SECRET! Everything you need is hidden inside of you like a buried treasure. You just have to remove the years of negativity and exfoliate the bad habits in order to commit to new good ones.

The first lesson I learned in my ability to Man Up was that I don't know everything and I should not pretend to. As the saying goes, "He that is his own doctor has a fool for a physician." Learn to draw from other experiences that are in relation to yours. The second lesson I learned was to change the way I viewed life. Someone said to me a long time ago, "Accept nothing without examination, reject nothing without consideration." With that in mind, I befriended a gentleman who motivated me to read more because his literature game was tight! And he would say to me, "If you're not reading and expanding your borders, people can tell you anything. They can either dazzle you with their brilliance, or baffle you with their B.S. But, without knowing for yourself, you won't be able to tell the difference!" I also met a woman on the job that opened my eyes to the world of working out and eating right. After sharing my struggles with her, she not only took the time to talk to me, she actually took me to the gym with her and helped me to understand the importance of guarding my temple. Eventually, my wings became strong enough to flap on my own. I took off and never looked back. I still thank God for their interventions to this very day!

I now weigh about 185 pounds. I have kept the weight off, I'm still married, and I'm still in the t-shirt business. I am also a coach of sorts, and a founding member of a company called Rejuvenetics. We put great emphasis on fighting free radical damage, and helping people live longer, feel better, and age gracefully through a concept called repair to perform. Adding Rejuvenetics to my daily regimen also played a role in me not relying on pharmaceutical medicine for the rest of my life, which as you know, can lead to death with long-term usage! Rejuvenetics is also a wonderful addition to building a healthy support system that complements a demanding lifestyle. There are too many people succeeding by committing to change for success to be labeled a secret. There's always information on what to do in order to get what you deserve, but rarely is there a discussion about undoing what was done to cause the drama. So, begin at ground zero in order to gain an advantage and build a legacy. This is a journey that we can take together. We just have to become sick and tired of being sick and tired, decide to go against the odds that have smothered our road to success, and strategically make adjustments for a better future. Man Up.

Chapter 20

Trend God

Sherrod Kersey

Introduction to Finding Myself

Throughout my life, I have always heard, "You are so talented." From as far back as I can remember, my creative talent always spoke volumes. Coming from New York City, a place of constant opportunity, I have often found finding my niche to be a double-edged sword; simultaneously easy and hard. My entrepreneurial spirit surfaced as a young boy, and during my childhood I was influenced by many aspects of my culture. Fortunately, my parents exposed me to a life of diversity which helped to mold my creative energy. Early on, I gravitated to sports, music, and fashion. These three outlets became the core of my interests. I was involved in numerous sports and played on various teams, I was always a fan of the most popular music, and I kept up with the latest fashion trends while creating my own.

As I continued my journey of self-exploration, determining what I would focus my energy on became difficult. My understanding of the concept that life's pursuit of success is a journey and not a destination posed challenges as I sought to hone in on the talents which would lead to my success. In my life, I've had plenty of jobs—dead-end jobs, temporary jobs, and even career opportunities. However, I have never put 100 percent into my own passion. I have always had an entrepreneurial mindset and desired to have my own business. I have spent a lot of time around artists (rappers, singers, people who played instruments). Creativity is very fascinating to me and has always had an impact on my life. Creativity and culture have shaped my life with fashion, music, and sports at the core. I can mostly relate to sports and fashion because I am very athletic and fashionable. Sports were my number one interest, but eventually, I lost that passion. At one point, I thought that I might want to pursue music, but I was never quite sure of what I wanted to do or what direction to go in musically. As a result of being around artists, I became interested in taking pictures. I assumed it was easy enough—just pick up a camera and start flicking. So, I started to learn a lot about cameras and specifically about a program called Photoshop. Mind you, I never went to any classes; but, once I learned that this program could be used to make photos look picture perfect, I started going on the internet and I did my own research. As I began researching more about this program, I realized that there are a lot of things you can do with photos. I learned about photo manipulation, graphics, logos, and all types of photo related information. I became so intrigued that I continued to research and found out that you could make logos, business cards, and flyers on Photoshop. I was blessed and gifted enough to be a quick learner which is almost a gift and a curse simultaneously. A curse because I can get sidetracked because of my interest and intrigue. It was life changing discovering that this program would allow me to learn different aspects about professional photography. So, I found myself pursuing photography as a business.

One day while I was working in Photoshop, I was asked if I knew how to make logos. Truthfully speaking, I did not. However, the combination of me needing extra dollars and my passion to produce graphic logos gave me the motivation to take a risk. As it turned out, the individual liked the logo and he requested that I put the logo on a shirt. That was a aha moment for me because it was during that project that I realized I wanted to make a clothing line. Sometimes the skills that you possess and all that you learn throughout the years is information for your purpose. I have been a sales man, a photographer, and a marketer. It became crystal clear to me that I had been placed in those positions to learn specific skills to fulfill my passion.

Proving Myself to Myself

Once I discovered my true passion, various challenges began to surface. Where am I going to get support from? What am I going to name my brand? What will be my overall target market? Questions and challenges went on and on and on. It was pretty interesting how I figured out the name of my brand. My first logo had three rings and wings, but it just did not do it for me. It literally took me one year to figure out the name of my brand. I began to show my logo to other people, and with modifications it began to take on a Trinity feel. As I pondered the Trinity approach, I thought about Trend. I applied my creative energy to Trend, added ITY, and came up with TRENDITY. Trends that last forever. My new logo was a dominant T with five stars above it. Finally, it was complete.

Suited for Success

By this time, I started a new job working with kids through the Department of Education. I have always been active with kids since I was 14. As we are all well aware, working with kids takes a lot of energy. This job acted as a catalyst and motivator in terms of fueling my dreams and passion. I was able to present myself as a role model and show the youth that you can pursue anything you want. I faced a lot of challenges in terms of support. Sometimes when somebody has a dream and there's nothing tangible to back it up, it's hard to believe in it. Especially if it's your dream and not somebody else's. So, when I first presented my dream to multiple people, it was just an idea and I was hoping they would have blind faith. But, it wasn't that easy. There was even a time when I was going to give up on my dream; but, I had a good friend, @Shisefoe, who helped reignite my interest when I showed him one of my ideas. Sharing this idea with him helped me open a new collection in the TRENDITY brand called Cutthroat Amerika. I also teamed up with two partners, my friend Torry and my other friend Qwizzy. These individuals were not my peers; they were older than me and wiser. They both had backgrounds in managing businesses, and from the time we partnered we have not looked back. Not only did these people give me the motivation to strive for what I want; but, through it all, I also got a reconnection with my God. During my entire life, my mother has always promoted God and the concept of spirituality. I believe that without having some type of faith in a higher power, you may be blocking your blessings and going nowhere fast.

On Purpose

As I started practicing better living habits, in terms of mind, body and soul, I realized that you receive blessings toward the things that you really want. The good habits that I began practicing regularly gave me things that I had prayed for and more. This included the growth of my brand, respect from others, and the respect I ultimately began to have for myself. Suddenly, everything got real. At first, most of my designs were straight computer-based. I was not getting any material and I wasn't getting hats, shirts, or clothing made. I was just fine-tuning my skills and my graphics. But, I began to research how to actually make my designs and my customized clothing. Now, the clothing industry is a funny game. You're going to have the people that give you good advice and you're going to have the people that give you no advice. You're going to have some real strong links and of course you are going to have some real week links. It's awkward when you ask people for help, especially when you're in the same field as they are. Personally, I feel like each one teach one. If I were at the top of a wall, I would put my hand down and pull the next person up. I feel that if we make it, we are obligated to bore a hole in the wall and pull someone else through. However, I live in New York City where everybody is hustling and multiple people are going to have the same hustle as you. Of course, with me being a rookie, I had to go out and ask people in my field (that I knew and didn't know) to show me the ropes. Needless to say, the different responses I received ranged from good to bad. I had people who gave me great information and great links as well as the opposite. Sometimes people feel like if they give you their "secrets" on how they made it, you could become a threat. I have the kind of mindset that tells me that if someone is blessed with something, they should share the blessing. I believe that God blesses us so that we can be a blessing to someone else.

Due to some of the information I was getting from certain people, I realized that I had to lace up my boots and do my own footwork. I spent hours upon hours on YouTube, figuring out how to start up a clothing brand. I sacrificed days just to go down to the Fashion District to explore and gather information. I spent a lot of time trying to perfect my craft. As I got more versed in the clothing line field, I found the resources necessary to start making clothes. Remember that as a man who was attracted to fashion design, I just woke up one day with a burning desire and vision to start my own business. I came to the realization that if you wait or depend on anybody for anything that you want or need, you might be waiting forever. I refuse to put my dreams into somebody else's hands. As I progressed, the same people who I asked for help started asking me where I got my stuff done. Within a couple of months, I had snapback hats, t-shirts, sweaters, etc. One of my most famous designs is my American flag razor. I took a razor blade and put the American flag on it, with the flag dripping blood. Now, this might sound vulgar, but most of my graphics send a message. When you see this design, it could be interpreted many ways. However, what I've noticed the most about this design is that it evokes respect from a variety of people of all races and age groups, especially when I tell them what it represents. It's even kind of crazy when people see it and I don't have to explain its meaning because they automatically know where I'm coming from. However, here is the breakdown of that design. I actually made it while watching the news around the time that Eric Garner died due to an officer's chokehold because he was selling cigarettes. It was also during the time that Future had his famous song called "March Madness." The song relayed a message about everything that was going on in March 2015. This razor design which opened my collection, Cutthroat Amerika under TRENDITY, spoke volumes about what was going on in America. This collection is not intended to be focused on racism or race. This design is intended to send a message about the kind of country we are living in today. I am proud to be able to live in a land where I have opportunity, but it doesn't mean I'm not fully aware of the things that go on. I have to work twice as hard to make a living because of being a black male in America. Race is not at the core of my design because I've met multiple people from different races, creeds, and places that can attest to the fact that we live in a Cutthroat America. The cutthroat tactics could be in terms of job opportunity, treatment of people, housing, education, etc. I am taking the opportunity to express America's cutthroat tactics through fashion.

The feedback from the design was tremendous. It came to the point where every time I saw someone, they asked for some kind of clothing. My team was getting similar feedback, and my social media started to reflect what I was promoting. It was a wonderful feeling to see a plan come to fruition. Next thing you know, I began to make small Instagram videos and promotional posts. It was a lot for me to handle. Thank God I had my team. I relied on my team for promoting, marketing, capital, and getting the word out. My team definitely held me down. However, when it comes to marketing creativity, which includes the photos and designs, that all falls on my shoulders. My first full year passed. And although it wasn't the best year, it established that we have a product that people want. The biggest challenges we had was that the demand was higher than the supply and financial management. Now, I am currently in my second year and a lot has transpired. My clothing is being seen in different boroughs, different cities, and even different states. I have sponsored youth basketball teams and provide celebrities with my own apparel. I have been invited to attend and participate in fashion shows and have even done a couple of pop-up shops. The TRENDITY brand is still growing, and we are looking forward to having longevity in the fashion industry.

The main point I wanted to convey in this chapter is that you have to believe in your dreams because they are yours not anybody else's. You have to put the footwork in, enjoy the good times, and persevere through the tough times. First and foremost, you must believe in yourself. I'm grateful, and I thank God every day for blessing me with the talent I possess. I am provided with grace and mercy every day that I wake up, and that is not my will but His. Today, not only am I a good friend and family member, but I have also tried to be a great role model for the youth. I'm proud to be an educated, motivated black male, and I feel obligated to set an example and be on the front line of a positive movement.

Chapter 21

Mentoring

Darrell J. Edmonds

"It is easier to build strong boys than to repair broken men." —Frederick Douglass

To fully understand why I've been suited for success, you must first understand who and what suited me. Growing up in a small town with a large family, my environment was very controlled. As a teen, it felt constricting because I always wanted to have the same freedom as my peers. They seemed to be able to make decisions for themselves and experience more. Looking back, I see that much of what they experienced was unhealthy and the restrictions that I lived under were in place for my own protection. Even though I wasn't always comfortable with the structure, the benefits outweighed the complaints. Everywhere I looked, I was surrounded by strong examples. I never had to go far to find someone that was modeling responsible behavior. The prime among those examples was my father. He was a stalwart in our family. I am the third of his four children; so, I only suffered from a mild case of middle child syndrome.

My father and mother raised us in a loving, caring home with strong Christian values. Those values undergirded every facet of our home. Every Sunday, without exception, one could find our family in worship at Union Baptist Temple in Atlantic City, N.J. My father would be seated on the front row, on the left-hand side of the sanctuary, with the deacons. My mother sat only a pew or two behind him with the deaconesses. As their children, we were also in place with the children's choir or young adult choir. I was seated at the piano since I was 11 years old. After church, we would have dinner as a family, including the occasional fish fry at my maternal grandmother's home who lived across the street from us. When we gathered there, you could find all of her children and grandchildren huddled around the pot to get a piece of fish hot out of the grease. Even as a very young child, I can remember family Bible studies in that same house. Holidays were all of this plus more. I can remember a house full of 30 or more people on Thanksgiving. Relatives and friends from all over

Suited for Success

would come through to fellowship and partake in some of the good food. My story is not one with a tragic, troubled childhood. Actually, it was quite the opposite. I was surrounded by love, support, and family.

Among those who loved me deeply where the men in my life. There was no shortage of male role models in our neighborhood. There was my maternal grandfather. A WWII veteran, church deacon, and jack of all trades. My grandfather was like Superman to us. He could build anything, including five of the houses in our neighborhood. He could shoot a groundhog with a shotgun from 50 yards away, aiming from his bedroom window down to his garden where that pest had attempted to enjoy the collard greens before we had a chance to. Mr. Goodrum was one of our neighbors. He wasn't a relative, but he might as well have been. He was a nationally ranked power lifter, little league coach, and school board member. Mr. Goodrum was my little league baseball coach and made sure that we all got to and from practices during baseball and football seasons. Then there was my Uncle Bill. He was a church deacon, city council member, and our version of Joe Jackson. Uncle Bill made sure that our family band rehearsed and got around to gigs. Yup, we had a singing group called Cousins and later it was called Divine Connection. In my life, chief among all these men was my father. Jesse Edmonds Jr. was a church deacon, school board president, and Omega man. He was loving and kind, yet authoritative and stern. He had a voice that you could hear call you from across the street, as well as change the way you felt about a hymn forever when he sang in church. My dad was not just a man. He was "the man" to me, my siblings, and many others that came into contact with him.

My father was a social worker at Atlantic City High School, and somehow his duties included handing out lunch tickets. Throughout my life, I've heard countless stories from people about how he made sure they were fed and even counseled them through tough times in high school. As much as he served others and his community, he was consistent with our family. He was an example in how he loved our mother and showed her his devotion and admiration daily. His love for his children was an extension of how he felt about his wife and our mother. There was nothing lacking. These are the people and the conditions that suited or prepared me for success. I realize that I am blessed to have what I did.

One day, while talking with one of my mentees shortly after my father passed, I was explaining how I had peace because my life was full of experiences with my father, love from my father, and the example he lived out for us to see. That young man said in response, "All that fullness you feel… for me is emptiness because I didn't have what you had." That response truly put my experience into context and helped me to better understand some of the pain these young men deal with. It was as plain as day in that moment. I was quiet for a minute because I was kind of in my feelings, having just lost my father and sharing all that he meant to me. That young man explained that part of him is empty, not just because his father wasn't in his life, but he also articulated that there was a lack of men to step in and fill some of the role. Furthermore, there was an anger that resulted and eventually filled up those empty places. I was presented with an opportunity. To be honest, I didn't have a response immediately. This was something that I had to sit with for a couple of days. At the time, I was in year two of building a small, local mentoring program. Mentoring was natural for me because, as I have shared, I had such powerful models in my own life. However, that young man's response caused me to question if I was adequate in that role. I didn't know what it was like to not have a father or a "village" of men involved in raising me.

After much prayer and discussion, the answer came to me crystal clear: I cannot give something that I don't already have. My experience prepared me to give to this young man and others what was given to me. I was even reminded of the fable of the eagle who lived as a chicken. It wasn't until he finally saw an eagle one day that the misguided eagle could learn to fly and truly live as an eagle himself.

Mentors play a huge role in our community. They are able to help young men and women overcome the uncertainty and fear we all face while chasing our goals.

Chapter 22

The Latter Shall Be Greater
Dimitri David Jr.

"So I will restore to you the years that the swarming locust has eaten...
You shall eat in plenty and be satisfied."
—Joel 2:25-26 (NKJV)

It is said that "Rome was not built in a day," but what is to be said about a life that was by all measures a successful one until challenged by the instrument of failure? This is the question I often ask myself when I think about my journey to success. Life can be funny, and what one may set out to accomplish may only be a thing of the imagination. What I have discovered in my pilgrimage is to remain humble and keep God at the center. While we can strive to be intentional in our pursuits, it is wise to give room to understanding our limitations and learning to lean on the one who is greater, trusting Him with our future. There is something that needs to be said about fearing God and growing in the knowledge of self. The Scripture teaches that it's when we fear God that wisdom emerges. Furthermore, trusting God and surrendering our future to Him is what's going to bring a sense of purpose and fulfillment. At times, life can throw curve balls at us and if we're not rooted in our pursuit to fulfill our dreams, we can drown by the trials and tribulations that come. As a matter of fact, true strength and success are measured by how an individual deals with resistance against their dreams. When passion and commitment are interwoven in the character of a man or woman, no trial or adversity can hinder the drive to accomplish an objective or meet a goal.

Passion is a powerful resource in the life of an individual. It's the impetus that keeps a person moving forward toward their dreams. When a man is robbed of his passion, a sense of lethargy sets in and drains his desire to accomplish his objectives, especially when there are challenges and trials. This is a reality I know all too well given my divorce and role as a religious leader in my community. It was hard having to remain silent and take criticism from many who didn't know anything about my situation. But because I was a figure of authority, I had to be perfect. Anything short of that made me unworthy as a pastor and leader. It was difficult leading a congregation of people who didn't know the details of my ordeal or understand the emotional pain I was facing. What made it worse were the many things that were said about me that were not true. Having to stand every Sunday and speak about the standards of Christian living knowing my own challenges was trying. It was at those moments that I realized the significance of my own humanity. I also learned humility and tolerance. I must admit that I was always sensitive to the imperfections of men, but after my divorce I developed a greater sense of grace for people who had fallen or may not be where they desire to be in life. Too many times, the church is callous when it comes to the hurting and the downcast. Many times, when an individual falls or is misunderstood, the church often throws that individual away without remorse. The people of God in their self-righteousness often forget the very words of Jesus when He said, "Forgive your neighbor." We are so quick to remember the wrongs and fail to realize that we all have sinned or fallen short in some area. I'm not saying that I shouldn't be an example of righteousness, for I truly believe that it was my duty as a leader to live out my Christian experience the best way I knew how; but, when it came to expecting sympathy from others, I didn't get that from most. So, while I understood why people had concerns about my divorce, I felt discouraged by the lack of understanding from the few who stood against my ministry and humanity. What I did find interesting was that in the subsequent years, many of the naysayers and spectators had various trials of their own and a number of people called to apologize to me about their insensitivity.

Within five years, my ministry experienced significant loss in membership and the cloud of failure shrouded my consciousness. All of my goals and aspirations were suddenly starting to look dim. My sense of pride in the work of ministry weakened. I began to see myself as a failure. In all honesty, I realize now that my greatest challenge was not the voices of the naysayers or even the downsizing of my congregation, but the image I started having of myself. That image was what ultimately kept me in the shadow of failure. What I had to do as an overcomer was to start seeing myself as a success, despite the setback. Having a poor self-image and feeling sorry for yourself can knock the wind out of you. I have come to realize that no matter what it is you're going through or the failure in your life, the journey is not over. As long as there is breath

Suited for Success

in your body and a mind to imagine, the sky is the limit.

At times, life can be unpredictable and challenging; but, that should never stop us from pursuing our goals. Passion and a healthy dose of confidence can take an individual very far. One example that comes to mind is that of Joshua and Caleb in the Bible. Here were two individuals among twelve men who were given the task to spy out the Land of Canaan at the command of Moses to see if it was fitting to inhabit. After returning to Moses and the people who numbered possibly over one million according to most biblical scholars, ten of the twelve men expressed that the land was good but that it would be impossible to possess it because the people inhibiting the land were like giants. In other words, they saw themselves as insignificant and incapable of taking the land. Only Caleb and Joshua had a different report.

> "Then Caleb silenced the people before Moses and said, 'We should go up and take possession of the land, for we can certainly do it.'" When the people complained that they could not go up to conquer the land, both Caleb and Joshua responded strongly: "Joshua son of Nun and Caleb son of Jephunneh . . . tore their clothes and said to

the entire Israelite assembly, 'The land we passed through and explored is exceedingly good. If the Lord is pleased with us, he will lead us into that land, a land flowing with milk and honey, and will give it to us. Only do not rebel against the Lord. And do not be afraid of the people of the land, because we will devour them. Their protection is gone, but the Lord is with us. Do not be afraid of them.'" (Numbers 13:30, 14:6-9, NIV; www.gotquestions.org).

Caleb and Joshua had a different attitude and did not let the size of those inhabitants in the land of Canaan intimidate them. It is noteworthy to state that anytime a new season or territory is on the horizon, there will always be opposition. But, if we are going to be successful in life, we must have the same attitude as Caleb and Joshua. Failure in our past or shortcomings in our present never have to dictate our future. I once heard someone say, "We need to use our mess as fertilizer for the soil of our future." God and divine providence have a way of restoring the time our mistakes and ignorance have robbed us of. God specializes in making that which appears weak (the underdog) the premier example of greatness. We must learn to never put a period in the various seasons of our lives where God has placed a comma. The story of our lives does not end with a setback or failure. We must remember that God has the last word. Never giving up and pressing toward the mark is our responsibility as long as we have life in our bodies. History has taught us, through the many figures in every genre of society, that persistence and resilience are what defines success and triumph.

The founder of Apple, Steve Jobs, is another example of what it means to be passionate and resilient about purpose. Back in 1976, Jobs was enthusiastic about the future of his company. Up until 1985 when he was fired from the company he helped start. Life sent Jobs a curveball he was not expecting, but it helped him grow and rise to greatness. After being fired, Jobs did not give up; he simply kept at it, starting the companies NeXT and Pixar. In 1996, the struggling Apple Company acquired the company NeXT and eventually made Steve Jobs CEO again. Back at the helm, Jobs was able to turn Apple Computer Company around creating the iPod, iPhone and iPad.

I opened this chapter with the famous quote, "Rome was not built in a day." This indicates that even in our season of famine when things are not going as we think they should, we ought to always work toward our passions and dreams.

When an individual is fused with vision, that will keep him moving. We must never lose vision based upon how things look. If I were to have quit when I started experiencing the backlash of my divorce, I would not be where I am today. The journey has been arduous and slow, but I'm still in route to my destiny. Having remarried and now pastoring a growing church, I have learned a lot about the process of laying brick by brick in the midst of adversity. The awesome power behind vision is not only what is seen, but also the sense of drive a visionary has when hope is in front of him. One of the things I have discovered about vision is that the one who possesses it never finds rest until that vision is realized. The Bible tells us, "Where there is no vision, the people perish" (Proverbs 29:18, KJV). Understand that money, influence, and resources are all important, but if there is no vision, all the things in the world will render an individual nothing. Fulfillment and true satisfaction are attained when we are fulfilling our God-given purpose, anything short of that is meaningless.

Our lives are like a film roll. Every event and season is a part of the film or journey to destiny. The latter shall be greater when we realize that the camera is still rolling. Regardless of the situations we encounter in our lives, if we can imagine and create, vision will serve as a magnet propelling us forward toward our goals. Our vision for the future will attract the necessary resources we need to be successful.

One of the greatest promises about the reality of hope is that it always points to the future. God does not measure His plan and power in your life by your limitations. Instead He measures the willingness of your "yes" to His purpose. I like what the Chinese philosopher Confucius said about never giving up, and I leave it with you: "It does not matter how slowly you go so long as you do not stop."—Confucius (551-479 BC)

Chapter 23

What Came First, the Growth or the Pain?

Cyriac St. Vil

It feels good when you realize you have just weathered a major storm that in prior instances would have knocked you off your feet. By keeping yourself firmly planted, and rooted in mantra and mission, you were not lost in this storm of death, sickness, defeat, or debt. Everyone has those moments. Your heroes do too. They have just figured out how to keep their momentum and get back into peak performance ("flow"). I, Cyriac St. Vil, sure have. And at this moment, I can only claim (hopefully) to be my wife and children's hero.

What enabled me to keep the mind state and trajectory of a man on a path to success are the tools, steps, and resources that propelled me through tough times and kept me focused when vices and vanity could possibly have derailed a life meant for abundance. As a child, I had no idea I was slowly shaping who I wanted to become as I acquired the necessary practices to assure my progress. I did know that the pains I felt was growth, the mistakes I made were to be learned from, and nothing in this life is a waste of time. As I've developed and matured, my faith in mankind and my positive outlook have allowed me to not get too down on myself. I know that I have the same thing YOU have—the ability to be successful when given a chance and access to opportunity. The first chance that needs to be given is from you to yourself. Give yourself every opportunity to win! Create every competitive advantage allowable.

These chances need to be facilitated by massive paradigm shifts. I stumbled upon every step to massive change that I encountered. This is not your average rags to riches story, mostly because my proud mother and father (of the Haitian diaspora) made my childhood far from one of rags. We weren't rich (my mom would often say we were poor people), but we had a warm, loving home with plenty to eat. And although they weren't the newest, we had clean clothes on our backs. My mom taught me the diligence and faith to move a mountain, pebble by pebble. My father taught me pride, strength, and to be a man amongst men. This is also not a rags to riches story for I have yet to reach material riches. My success is one of family, friends, happiness, and the path to all that life has to offer me. Here is my story of growth and pains that led me to my path of success.

Deter Some, Welcome Others via Physique

Going into 2001, my life was about operating a small business from the basement of a building, and partying with my friends and a hot girlfriend. It was a lifestyle that was heavily influenced by marijuana and a vegan diet. At 6'0" and 145 pounds, I was far from an imposing figure. I was willowy at best with dreadlocks that ran past my shoulders. Up to that point, my guile, ability to talk to people, and hard work had been more than enough to carry me through most of the situations life had thrown my way. At the beginning of 2001, at the age of 26, I got what I had long aspired for. I became, with two partners, a young owner of one of the largest and most well-known pet stores in NYC. It was a challenge that took every bit of everything I had to help build it from scratch and maintain it day to day. This new endeavor broke me down and lifted me up all in the same day, eight days a week, financially and otherwise. Some saw me as a super successful guy that made it, and others saw my success as a reason to test me in every way possible. "Is he lucky?" "Is he making real money?" "Can we muscle in on his business?" I was mentally ready, spiritually tough, and physically fit, but my stature was not a commanding one. My shoulders slumped, my chest was chicken-esque, and I looked to be the little brother of my bigger framed partners. I never felt small next to them. But, two things that are very really and have immediate impacts are first impressions and raw physicality. It was common place that those looking to throw their weight around would come to me first, as if to pressure the weakest link. It wasn't until four or five years later, when we finally went our separate ways and dissolved the business, that I took inventory and saw my physique as a flaw. The first step for me was recognizing that I did not like the idea that I wasn't my best in that area of my life.

I fervently read up on various workout regimens and diets, and went into depth on how to schedule workouts into my day and make them a part of my fabric. My first workout was 10 sets of 10 push-ups. I eventually worked my way up to 10 sets of 75. Along the way, I learned discipline, improved my time management, and proved to myself that I could make a change in my life. Years later, and 40-45 pounds heavier, I am completely content with my physique, and more importantly my presence when I enter a room. Remember every competitive advantage is to be used. If the best offense is a good defense, I found that a broad chest and muscle tone can create enough pause to assuage unneeded discrepancies. I lost a business and a dream but gained the idea of competitive advantage!

My second massive paradigm shift began in 2006. I had reestablished myself in business as a cable contractor with a crew of six guys. I was making great money and I had a good lady (a different one from last time). I still had growing to do, I still felt like I had things to prove, and I was still dancing with the devil in way too many ways. One of those ways was that I was still holding on to a habit I had since I was 17 years old—smoking marijuana. I smoked a lot of it, and I thought I would never stop. Another dance routine me and the devil had was the idea that most disputes could get handled via violence. Those two ideals came to a head on an evening when I stepped out to a party.

The outing was a bad idea on too many fronts to count. It was a humid New York City night in August, and the streets were alive with a very young college crowd. My girlfriend at the time was 21, and it was a mix of some of her friends and associates. I paid the possible imminent danger no mind because I was ready to defend myself. I figured I would smoke a little bit and all would be well. Unfortunately, we were with another couple that had some form of dysfunction in their pairing, and they were separated just enough for the guy to get jealous of other men dancing with his lady. Classic stuff. Picture *Carlito's Way*. Stupid, but classic. So, he exacerbates a bad situation and makes it worse by jumping into some guys face and started a fight. I jump in, and shortly thereafter we are fighting 10-15 guys in a free for all. Club security breaks it up and everyone hurriedly exits the club.

Better judgment would have told me to leave, better advice would have told me never to have been there. Instead, I stayed out in front and continued the fight against this large group of young men by myself. They didn't come out that night to attack me. It was a bad situation asking to get worse. I was in the middle of it, smelling like weed, very rough around the edges, and ready to fight, with a young girlfriend that could not have affected change at all. After the dust settled, I was stabbed twice. Once in my back, puncturing my lungs, and once in my neck, inches from a major artery. I definitely saw my life flashing before my eyes. I vividly remember seeing the crimson pools of blood forming on the ground after soaking my brand-new Dickies outfit. I would have died if not for an angel in the form of a passerby that descended upon me. While everyone that I knew was screaming and crying, a white guy came out of nowhere and put pressure on my neck so that I would not bleed out. At first, it felt like he was choking me, but he told me he was there to help. He didn't know anything about me. Not my name, if he was being exposed to a communicable disease, nothing. Yet, he saved me. He kept the pressure on my neck until the ambulance came, then he disappeared. I will tell you this, not a soul can ever typecast a race to me because that white guy was one of the best, most caring people I have ever met. I don't even know his name. I remember getting to the hospital and thinking, "Thank God my dick still works." I don't even know how I knew this, but it did. And after one week, I was back home recuperating. I did not hold on to the anger from being stabbed, but I did hold on to the lessons: I should not have been in that environment, those young men should have recognized me for the king I am, I was not representing myself properly, the people I was around were overwhelmed by the moment, and I was too quick to fall back into the default mode of violence.

While healing, I truly reintroduced myself to appreciating life. I started building and flying kites, cooking, reading, and taking long walks. I will never forget a moment during that summer when I was home resting and watching what was a great baseball game. The Mets had a rookie first baseman named Mike Jacobs. He had a lot of power and a great future. He could have been a contender. He hit a walk-off home run to win the game, and I started crying like a baby. I was happy for him. Happy I was alive to witness the moment. I was just happy. That surreal happiness followed me to when I got back on my feet. I got right back to business and working out as if not to miss a beat. I left behind the thoughts of that fight and the rough edges I was carrying around.

I decided I would represent myself in a better fashion, so I went clean cut and dressed more business casual. More importantly, I could not smoke while my lungs were healing. But, when I was cleared to smoke, I didn't want to. I didn't want the smoke, I didn't want the smell, I didn't want what came with it. Getting stabbed and almost losing my life improved my life because of how I reacted to it all. It is never what happens that changes your life, it is truly how you react and rebound. That was when I began to realize I could not be with that young lady either. It was a me thing and not about her. I needed to change my room (referring to the saying, "If you are the smartest person in the room, find a new room"), and I hadn't realized I had begun. It must've been something I wanted without knowing. It came through association with people that had different views on life than I was used to hearing and the networks that were built from those relationships. Some of the change took form in steps such as: chasing fast times and vanity less and building value through educating myself. A vast amount of value was added through my commitment to being of service to others, which allowed me to understand how much I had and how much I had to be grateful for. I also took stock in my place in the world and the relationships I had with both family and friends.

After that inventory, I saw that I needed to step into the role of someone that was able to act and speak differently than those around me. I embraced gaining knowledge from my elders, I gained insight from individuals I would have never previously listened to, and I learned not to put myself in the box created for me by the environment I was in. When I did this, I met people that shared resources

I had not been privy to, I learned of ways to allow prosperity into my life, and I found that there was so much I was missing on the other side of where I was. Where was I before? I was locked into the phenomenon of group thought and glass ceilings. I was locked in rooms where I couldn't grow. I was denied access to opportunity due to my mindset.

At that point in my life, I had already started multiple businesses, but I had never had an ounce of real financing or financial literacy training. I had many jobs, but I had never received a tax return or applied for a job that would build a pension or 401K. I had many relationships, but I never seriously considered having children or moving in with a girlfriend. As I began to study the serious people I was surrounded by, and put away bad habits and poor choices, all that was out of reach became attainable. I learned to treat my $10.00 the same way a millionaire treats his $1,000,000.00, with respect and like it means something. I learned that despite the roadblocks in the way of a black man in the United States of America, I can legally prosper in every way with a good plan and the right mind state. These revelations did not come all at once. They trickled in as I made better decisions. I chose solid individuals to associate with, which led to innumerable amounts of positive networking that continued to pay off. I instituted certain conditions on my behavior, such as: "Being late is childish." "If you don't trust the process of your to-do list, you don't trust yourself. Just do it." "Support your support system." "Cherish your loved ones." "Always do your homework and background work before important moments." "If there is a choice between dressing up or dressing down, always dress up and raise the bar."

My last major move and biggest paradigm shift was my change in outlook. It rearranged my thoughts, what I wanted to be around, and what I expected of myself. Mantra's are one of the resources I found to keep focused and on mission. I would always remember, "Thoughts become words and words become actions." As my outlook changed and my associations grew, another chapter began in 2010. In that year, I met my future wife, I started the job I am currently in management with, I finished the run of party promotions I was involved in, and I officially became a founding member of 500 Men Making a Difference. None of these occurrences seemed attached, but they all had one common thread—I began to change my room. My physique was solid and my outlook was where it needed to be; but, what was poured into my life that year is what I subconsciously called for. The change in room was not just my address (I moved in with my wife), or where I got my money (I maintained my business, but also got a job). It was the shift toward a room of stability, abundance, and constant growth through challenge. With each aspect, I was asked to compartmentalize what I had known all my life and use what I needed but make space for all I would learn and become. Upon embarking on these tasks, I knew it was a different world, so I sought out resources that could help me navigate the new terrain. These resources were:

1. Listening to podcasts such as: *The School of Greatness* by Lewis Howes. I amassed tons of insight from amazing people from all walks of life, and I was introduced to the idea of abundance.

2. Seeking out life lessons from in person connections or reading and watching videos. Countless people have mentored me without knowing. I was going to get those lessons TODAY!

3. Taking my losses as lessons. Whenever I swam in the deep end of the pool and almost drowned, I used that experience to learn what I did wrong and improve on it for the next opportunity.

4. Using short mantras to keep me focused. Three or four words I could repeat and follow when I was not sure of my next move for the day, week, or month.

5. Goal-setting and a to-do list. Since I was on this next level, I had next level responsibilities and next level goals. So, I began to set one big yearly goal and use weekly to-do lists to keep me focused. I learned that if you don't trust your own to-do list, you don't trust yourself. Your to-do list is you being your own task master. Listen to yourself.

These moves changed the functions I attended (more galas, meetings, and fundraisers than parties), the top ten people I spent most of my time with, the way I spoke and dressed, and the events I attended. I'm sure that my new habits had some close to me wondering if I changed. But, I only realized that I changed my room as I was writing this chapter.

There are two things I have conquered that have probably been the most important and will carry me for the rest of my life. First, never allow anything (besides your personal health) to slow you down or zap your energy. As long as you have a body that is able, all else can be worked on, worked out, created, or fixed. You are never out of the game as long as you have breath in your lungs. You must know and feel this with all your heart. Second, protect your heart and well-being with all your power and might. Your physical and mental well-being are the foundations of your success. Never take them for granted. You have in your hands the ability to actively formulate thoughts and ideas and execute them. Situations may dictate the speed or veracity of your movement toward your thoughts and ideas, but you have access to opportunity. If you are healthy and dead broke, you can still smile, laugh with your friends, and enjoy your hobbies; but, if deathly ill and stinking rich, you can do nothing of the sort. Every day is an amazing gift and we now live in such an amazing time. Most amazingly, it is your time. Do with it as you will; but, DO SOMETHING. Success is waiting for you.

Chapter 24

Metamorphosis: Transforming Yourself into What You Need to Become

Conrad W. Higgins

It was December 18, 1983, when my mother, younger brother, and I landed in New York City at John F. Kennedy International Airport from Jamaica, West Indies. The brisk, cold night was something I was not used to coming from a place that has year-round tropical weather; so, you can imagine the drastic change I experienced. Shuffling through the crowds, we began to take our journey to our new home. As we drove, I looked out the car window and saw the glitter of the city lights and the smoke of the winter air. I wondered what this new place was like and what new adventures lay ahead, then I began to look back at my time growing up in Jamaica and what I had left behind.

You see, as a kid I was very curious and had an adventurous imagination. Like most kids (boys), I loved to dig in the ground searching for lost treasure or build things like makeshift homes and objects from clay that I would extract from the soil. I would imagine that I was creating little cities and neighborhoods with the objects I found. Looking back, I always knew I was a creative child, but never knew to what extent. My parents never had the resources to send us to arts and crafts school or swimming classes (you know, the things we now do for our children) because their resources were reserved to take care of the six kids they had. Nevertheless, that didn't stop my willingness to be adventurous and always observant in my surroundings. The times we are living in today have sure changed from when I was growing up; imagination has been replaced by technology. The willingness to be creative without any triggers from the outside world has slowly diminished to the point where we as a society are captivated by other people's dreams and visions rather than our own.

So, how did I get to be a business CEO and broker for a fast-growing real estate firm in East New York, Brooklyn? How did a young Jamaican boy who had no idea what "America the Great" was about and who had to deal with so many

Suited for Success

obstacles as a child in this new country reach this far? How did a young man, growing up in the latter part of his teenage years without a father, climb the ladder of success and achieve all that he is doing now? How is he still pressing for bigger things? Well, it started with one of the things I love, which was to watch the development of housing communities and people making additions to their homes in our community back in Jamaica. I had a deep infatuation with construction and the thought of building something from nothing. To my remembrance, my first experience around construction was with my dad who was a bookkeeper for a big development company that built up the surrounding land areas into homes in my neighborhood and throughout Jamaica.

After arriving in the United States, that desire was put to rest for a brief moment. However, as I matured and relished my drawing and designing abilities, I started to look into architecture as a profession while in high school. My pursuit fell short when I lost my dad at 18 years old. I lost my desire to do what I wanted. For me, my mom and dad are everything, but my heart had a special place for my dad. So, when he died, it broke me into pieces and I just wanted to be left alone. I finished high school and went on to college. I majored in Liberal Arts because I wasn't sure anymore what to do and I didn't have any guidance. I flunked out my first two years and stopped going. I was in a place where I was left to my own devices without a plan or any help. But, one day when I was walking to church on a Sunday morning, feeling depressed and confused, I looked down and saw that my shoelace was untied. I reached down to tie it, and for some reason I looked across the street and saw a building that was so abandoned trees were growing out of it. The building caught my attention for the very first time in all my years living in that neighborhood. You see, I'd driven, walked past, and lived a few blocks from that building yet never noticed it the way I saw it that day.

That Sunday morning, something in me started to stir up. As I paused and looked at the building, I saw a multiplicity of ways I could make it a successful apartment building. I felt a drive in me like I've never felt before, and an overwhelming excitement came over me about that vast structure. I went on to church; but, when I should have been listening to the preacher, I was figuring out what my next step would be to get that building. I was about 21 years old, and deep down I knew I didn't have the money or the help to attain it. But, my imagination began to resurface. I realized that the first thing I needed to do was to find out more information about the building at the buildings department. Long story short, after my deep research, the building wasn't for sale and the city had no plans to sell it at that time. But, as the adage says, "If I knew then what I know now, things would be different." At the end of the day, you would think this would dash my hopes of one day becoming a successful business man and property owner; however, it did just the opposite.

At the age of 22, I began looking at buildings to buy and researching how to purchase them, which started to stir up that old desire to be my own boss one day. I said to myself, "I want to get into owning buildings and be in business." I didn't have any money or connections, but I knew what I wanted, and I had plans to build an empire from the ground up. So, I thank God for allowing me to see that building that day. It ignited the desire and drive in me once again to be an entrepreneur.

My dad and my mom were business-minded people who ventured out to be business owners. Some of their businesses failed and some were successful; nevertheless, they were always trying a new business idea to better themselves and our family. They never gave up, and I knew I shouldn't give up either. Your kids, family, and even strangers want to try something new and adventurous too; but, they are watching you to see if you can climb to the mountain top first. Many people are afraid to launch out and attempt to do something out of the ordinary. They are looking for an example as close to them as possible to emulate. Climbing to the top of your mountain may not be like there's, but they are watching the process it will take to get there. So, you have no time to slack off or lose hope. If your last business venture failed, dust yourself off and try again. This time, try to figure out these three things:

1. Why it failed.

    After you pick yourself up off the ground, take a step back and do an overview of your business. Analyze it. Ask questions of your family members and people who can give you an honest critique of your business. What could you have done better to achieve the success you desire?

2. How you can "tweak it" and get it back on track.

3. Did you put ALL that's in you into what you were doing?

Remember: A vision is going to go as far as the person seeing it. So, it's essential that your thoughts and heart are fully persuaded that you can get this done.

My parents weren't rich by any stretch of the imagination, but they had a plan to become well off. I remember when they wanted to own a grocery store (well, in my country we called it a shop). I would see my dad bringing home sand, cement, cinder blocks, and all the materials to convert our garage into this new shop for my mom to do their business. I saw them create a chicken coup, raise chickens, sell them to KFC, and became one of KFC's chicken providers. At one point, my dad owned a pig farm and a horse that he raced. I can go on and on, but they were trying a slew of things just to make something happen! How many of us think about what we want, but don't have the guts or the drive to make something happen? I remembered a while back a pastor said to me, "Son, if you want to survive in this country that is built on capitalism, you have to learn how to capitalize on something or someone will capitalize on you." You have to get off your rump, put what's in your head to paper, and bring it to life. It's not going to be easy.

For me, it took years to attempt to be an entrepreneur like my parents and build my own company. So, no matter how difficult it looks or how daunting it may seem to get your plans off the ground, always remember that many have failed, but only those who get back up and keep trying make it to the finish line. Even if those business ventures fail, try something else until you find what you're passionate about. I told some of my agents once that if you keep shooting at a target, even though you may miss most of the time, one of those arrows will eventually hit the mark. It's just a matter of time, practice, and patience. Some of you may not have guidance or parents to emulate, but successful people who have done it can be the inspiration to get you to the next level. The question I have for you is, "Are you willing to go through the metamorphosis process?" Are you willing to change some things about yourself to achieve what you really want in life? Because what you want isn't going to happen with you wishing and hoping. You have to be like the caterpillar. Put yourself in a cocoon and develop yourself into something new to get where you want to go.

There are four stages that take place during the metamorphosis phase for a caterpillar to become a moth or a butterfly. We will see how these stages manifest in business and entrepreneurship.

1. **Birth-** Some people are still at this stage of their life. They don't understand business, they don't know how business works, and they don't know how to do business from a pure place. Many people fail because they don't have the basic knowledge and understanding of business. Having a great idea doesn't necessarily mean you're going to be great at doing business. This stage is where you learn about integrity, trust, and most of all customer service. Many entrepreneurs lose sight of this stage because they want to get to the maturity stage and obtain all that it has to offer.

2. **Development-** This is when you hone in on your craft and your vision. Study, plan, and build yourself up. Stop hanging with sloths and learn how to fly like an eagle. As the old saying by Benjamin Franklin goes, "If you fail to plan, you are planning to fail."

3. **Growth-** Always do an evaluation of yourself, your business, and your goals. Check every part of your life and your business to see where it is. Do diagnostic

tests to make sure things are growing as you plan. Sometimes you have to let people or things go during this stage. A planter who has a garden has to keep constant tabs on the grass because in a garden weeds and grass can't grow together. Grass is designed to flourish while a weed is designed to stop the grass from growing. At the end of the day, you must determine who your weeds are and who your grass is.

4. **Maturity-** This is the final stage where you will now soar to a new level in your life. This is where you're not concerned about people's perception of you. You're not concerned about trivial stuff because you have reached a level of maturity where none of those things matter anymore. Maturity simple means you have grown up from the other three stages and now you are ready to fly around to new levels and new platforms while meeting new people who have the same mindset, drive, and passion as you. This is the stage where you will be able to tell the difference between the other stages. It takes a certain type of individual to move through the previous stages and get to this level while building a vision, a plan, and

keeping your sanity and integrity in check. Please understand that getting here does not mean you are done. This is only the beginning of many things to come.

Ultimately, your goal is to become a mature butterfly, soaring to be the BEST at what you do. Keep in mind that the road is not easy, and the weight can become heavy. But, once you become a butterfly, don't forget where you've come from. Always remember what it took to become you. It wasn't easy for me to become the butterfly I am now. But, I know that if my dad was still alive, he would see that I have taken the passion he had and metamorphosed into the businessman I am today. Write the vision and make it plan, but don't sit on it until it ends up in a grave. Sometimes you have to change who you are to get where you need to go.

Chapter 25

My Death Gave Birth to a New Me
Ty Brown

As I began to prepare for this amazing opportunity to join men in this project, I did what I normally do: I put some empty sheets of paper on the wall, took out some blank index cards, and began to outline main points with bulleted subpoints so that I could choose what to submit in my chapter. I'll admit, I struggled. Not because I didn't know what I wanted to say or what bullets were more powerful than others. I struggled with the fact that after days of outlining, something was missing!

So, I pushed myself away from the project, listened to some music and cleaned the house. Once the house was nice and clean, I finally went to bed. I am an early riser, normally up between 4:00 a.m. and 6:00 a.m. On the day I had to submit this project, I woke up at 9:00 a.m. I woke up with an answer. I finally decided what I would write about, and it didn't appear in any of the notes on the wall. It didn't show up on any of the index cards. Now that the decision was made and I was absolutely sure this was what I should write about, I couldn't stop the tears from flowing because I know why I ignored it for so long. I didn't want to step back. I didn't want to step in. I didn't want to remind myself.

Depression: The Dark Days

I was 13 when I was introduced to marching band. I fell in love. It is safe to say that was my first time in love! I loved leadership. I loved the opportunity to take an idea and make it grow. Think it, plan it, do it, and enjoy the accolades that came along with it. I was in love with goal-setting, in love with outshining the competition, and I was in love with SUCCESS! I was also determined. From ages 19 to 29, I was at the top of my field, and I had accomplished some amazing things. I grew one of the largest youth organizations in Brooklyn. It was nationally known and had partnerships with major corporations and political figures. I had two or three smaller companies that were also producing very good numbers and helping provide an amazing life for my wife and son. I worked hard, and I loved it. Working seven days a week was normal to me.

I got up, I got out, and I turned goals into WINS. Fueled by passion, I knocked down everything in my path! But, in 2009, I lost it all! All operations were closed, and that's when I met depression.

There were moments when I no longer loved myself. I was unsure of what to do, where to go and what was next. I recall, very well, not wanting to be alive anymore. I wanted to break away from the struggle and the pain. I felt embarrassed that my wife had to leave the house daily to go to work to provide for us. I felt like I was worthless and had no life purpose.

Depression, the result of the consequences of my poor choices, became my new hobby, my new job, and my new daily routine. It overtook me. It was in control, and it was strong. Depression dragged me into a deep dark hole with voices of self-doubt, self-hate and self-destruction. In this dark hole, they spoke loudly, even when they whispered. They spoke to me and told me I wasn't special, my life was over, I was a has-been, and I was never meant to be. The voices told me I made this bed and I was in this position because of my own doing.

Self-doubt was in the left corner. Because of it, I didn't think I was worthy. If I lived my life claiming band was my passion and now it was gone, taken away from me, what was the purpose of living?

Self-hate was in the other corner. He whispered thoughts of how horrible a person I was. He told me I was evil, deceptive, and a fraud. He told me I was fat and would always be fat. He shared stories related to my personal thoughts. I always wondered how he knew them. He heightened the volume of those thoughts and would always chime in, "You have these thoughts because that's who you ARE!" I believed him. I was scared that I was evil, and afraid that because I hated myself, who would ever love me?

Self-destruction was at the center of this hole of depression. In fact, he became the shovel that made the hole of my issues deeper. It was through self-destruction that I gave birth to new ways to hurt myself. It was this self-destructive voice that encouraged me to delve into other behaviors that caused me further problems.

I would wake up in the morning, after my wife and son had already left the house and close the dark curtains on the windows. I purposely wanted dark curtains and further engulfed myself in darkness by keeping them closed. I was afraid of the light, afraid of the cool breeze, and afraid of the sounds of birds. I made days my nights and

Suited for Success

I slept! I went from eating a breakfast sandwich on a regular roll to putting it on a long hero and adding ketchup and mayo. I gained weight and wound up reaching 260 pounds. I slept, woke up to eat, and slept some more. After a while, I had dark spots on my face and my skin tone changed. I didn't have a regular grooming schedule and I didn't care much about how I looked. I was sloppy, the house smelled stuffy when my wife came home, and I left dishes and other evidence of my day all over the house.

I had no drive, no desire, and I didn't care much about anything. I had friends who joined me in self-destructive behaviors. I created new bad habits, and some of my older ones were now prominent. All in all, there was a feeling that this was it. This was what I earned for myself and this was the new life I had built.

I began to hide my depressed state from my son by waking up early and getting dressed before he left the house. I saw him off and then went back to my routine. My wife encouraged me to get up and do something, and I would nod my head and say, "Ok." Others began to check on me, and I would nod my head and say, "Yes, I'm fine." But, no matter who called or spoke a positive word, I had to decide when enough was enough!

The time did come when I didn't want to be in that negative state anymore. So, the birth of Ty Brown began! I decided I had to kill Tyrone Brown and give birth to a new me. I began to leave the house again. I walked to the park where I loved sitting and watching the water. I enjoyed the sun and the wind again! I reconnected with church. I sat in the back of St. Paul's Community Baptist Church and cried from the first stroke of the piano to the last "Please stand before we dismiss." I wondered why I returned each week, knowing that all I would do was CRY! But, I felt amazing when I stepped out of church after each service and let that light of sun hit my face. I ran home and put on more gospel music as I planned my week of action. My plan of attack. I told myself that my comeback would be a story worth watching.

I began to share daily posts on Facebook and reconnect with people. I was transparent, and I asked others to hold me accountable for what I said I would do. I began to develop a voice, a brand, and an audience. I shared my daily movements and what powerful words were driving me. Affirmations and quotes became an everyday habit. Reading them and analyzing their meanings gave me the strength I needed. I started to dream again! I allowed my ideas to flow and then I aggressively pursued them. I learned that failures are lessons, and I went to class each day looking to win or learn. I believed that losing was also a lesson; so, I took the word out of my vocabulary. I told myself, "If I was at the top before, I can build back up to the top again!"

Passion and purpose never left me. I was living my truth when I said that band was my life's purpose and the reason I was placed on this earth. There was a burning desire in me to create a band again, and that I did!

As I began to rebuild, I still listened to the voices; but not the voice of self-doubt, self-hate, and self-destruction. This time, I listened to the voice of God who had become the loudest voice in my head. I began to allow our conversations to reign over my life. I began to allow His directions to be my marching orders and my daily "things to do" list. I began to put all my lessons into my tool bag, and it became full of instruments that I used to combat and kill negative behaviors and thoughts. Those tools helped me to build walls that not only protected me but allowed me to stand atop them to see things differently. I once weighed 260 pounds; today I weigh 210 pounds. I love getting dressed, putting on my favorite pieces of jewelry, and getting my hair cut regularly. I am renewed, revived, and rejuvenated.

Today, I have amazing businesses that will one day do over one million dollars in sales and programs that service over 500 families a year. Today, I am in love with an amazing woman with whom I choose to enjoy life. Today, I vacation when I'm ready, I take time for me when I want, and I still WORK HARD! Today, I love me, I respect me, and I make decisions with more integrity. I am transparent and aim to share my story. Today, I am powerful and stand strong in my truth that I may not be perfect, but my best days are ahead of me and my worst days have been destroyed. And over all, today I tell myself that I am a survivor of the chapter in my life called depression!

Prayer Against Depression

Depression, be gone! Depression, go away! Depression, you have no place in my life. You are a temporary lesson that I will learn from and move past! Depression may you serve your purpose while here, but do not get comfortable. I will not allow you to overtake me! My life is meant for greatness. My life is meant for good and delivers to my God I will!

Amen!

Sources

Unless otherwise indicated, scripture quotations are from the Holy Bible, King James Version. All rights reserved.

Scriptures marked ESV are taken from English Standard Version®. Copyright © 2001 by Crossway, a publishing ministry of Good News Publishers. All rights reserved.

Scriptures marked NIV are taken from the New International Version®. Copyright © 1973, 1978, 1984, 2011 by Biblica, Inc.™. All rights reserved.

Scriptures marked NKJV are taken from the New King James Version®. Copyright © 1982 by Thomas Nelson. All rights reserved.

About the Authors

PK Kersey is the founder of That Suits You, a nonprofit organization that provides suits to deserving men; partners with NYC schools to teach, train, and motivate young people; and offers training, presentations, and overall assistance with several certified job programs throughout NYC and beyond. He is also the founder of PKs Pitch, a blog that handles the social media activity for businesses across the United States.

PK has been named Black Enterprise's Modern Man, *NY1* New Yorker of the Week, and he has received the Young, Gift & Black entrepreneurial award. He also co-authored the book, *Renegotiating Greatness*.

Prior to founding his company, PK worked as a New York State employee for over 24 years. He has been married for over 25 years and is the father of twin boys. PK lives by the motto, "It is never lonely at the top, if you take people with you!"

Learn more at
www.thatsuitsyou.org

About the Authors

Shannon Lanier, a veteran television host, media personality, and author, has been keeping audiences tuned in his entire life. Shannon most recently co-hosted *Arise Entertainment 360*, a daily culture and entertainment series that aired on BET's sister station, Centric, and cable providers globally. *Arise Entertainment 360* was part of Arise News, a network seen in over 175 million homes in more than 50 countries throughout the world, including Europe, the Middle East, and Africa. Shannon is also known for his work as a correspondent and senior producer on Black Enterprise Magazine's nationally syndicated shows: *Black Enterprise Business Report* and *Our World with Black Enterprise*

Charles A. Archer is an American lawyer, author, speaker, advisor, entrepreneur, co-founder and CEO of The THRIVE Network. THRIVE assists thousands of individuals, throughout New York, with intellectual and developmental disabilities to live with dignity, respect, and independence. Charles's recent third book, *Everybody Paddles: A Leaders Blueprint for Creating a Unified Team*, is an international bestseller providing a management model focused on reaching strategic alignment and accelerating organizational change through respect, collaboration, and leadership.

Charles's enthusiasm about advocacy, community development, business sustainability, and policy reform has led him to receive a master's of public administration and pursue a PhD in public policy. In addition to his service on countless boards, Charles presented two TEDx Talks entitled "The Friendship Clause" and "IDENTITYphobia." He remains a Forbes and Huffington Post contributor and has been featured on television, radio, print, and other media outlets. Later this year, Charles will publish his fourth book.

About the Authors

Dr. Jean Alerte is an award-winning entrepreneur with a variety of work experience in the areas of marketing, management, and sales. Along with founding his company, ACA Branding Agency, he also serves as the executive director of Unity in the Community in Brooklyn, where he has given out $32,000.00 to high school students to attend college. He turned his first book, *Do Right, Do Good*, into the successful entrepreneurial program, FAITH GRIND INSPIRE, which teaches over 2,000 inner-city students entrepreneurship.

Originally from Port-au-Prince, Haiti, Alerte currently resides in Brooklyn with his wife, with whom he opened Brooklyn Swirl frozen yogurt shop in 2012, and their 17-month-old son. Dr. Alerte has been featured on ABC 7's *Here and Now* with Sandra Bookman, *BK Live*, NBC's *TODAY Show*, Fox, Arise, and in *Essence Magazine* highlighting his book, *Single Man, Married Man*.

Suited for Success

Jamael Thompson was born and raised in Brooklyn, N.Y. He is a proud husband and father of two girls, Isabella and Victoria. Having worked in the banking industry since 2005, Jamael has vast experience in business banking for a major financial institution in Midtown, Manhattan. Jamael received his degree in business economics from SUNY University at Buffalo, and obtained a certificate in credit analysis from NYUSCPS.

Having mentored young boys at his neighborhood Boys & Girls Club while in high school and tutored at a local elementary school while in college, Jamael continues to speak with inner-city elementary and high school students, encouraging them to strive for greatness and beat the odds. As the co-founder of That Suits You, a nonprofit organization, Jamael assists young men in obtaining suits, shirts, and ties for job interviews.

About the Authors

Aaron S. Jenkins, MHS-C is a counselor with a background in public speaking and organizational management. His journey has afforded him the opportunity to be a facilitator for several community-based organizations within the tri-state area.

Under the mentorship of Dr. A. R. Bernard Sr., Aaron is a staff member at Christian Cultural Center located in Brooklyn, N.Y. He has also been a fellow of Derek Suite, M.D., and the CEO and co-founder of Full Circle Health, an outpatient behavioral health and training resource.

With a heart for community, Aaron established the R.C.E. Group (Restoring Community Excellence), an organizational resource designed to revolutionize the relationship experience through one-to-one and group collaborative efforts.

Randall E. Toby is the founder of the Magnificent Men Mentoring Group, which serves youth and adult males by providing workshops, seminars, and performing community service. He was also the co-founder of International Entertainment Network which managed famed New York radio DJ, John Robinson, DJ Juan Coon, and renowned video chorographer, Shake.

Randall has over 10 years of experience as a corporate sales professional for organizations such as: American Express, Verizon Wireless, and Sprint. He spent over five years as a training and education manager for a workforce development company where he coached and trained individuals seeking to gain employment. In addition, Randall has served as a motivational and keynote speaker for the Brooklyn Probation Department, TEP Charter School, Berkeley College, Harlem Youth Marines, Rikers Island Correctional Facility, the New York County District Attorney's Office, the Metropolitan College of New York, the STRIVE program, Samaritan Village, and Middle School 256.

About the Authors

Dr. Oliver T. Reid, a native of Charlotte, North Carolina, is married and a proud father. Dr. Reid graduated from Winston Salem State University with a B.A./B.S. degree in history and sociology and earned a master's in theology from Life Christian University. He obtained his PhD in Christian counseling from Clarity International University, and provides consulting and coaching services.

In 2013, Dr. Reid launched I Am A Solution Consulting Firm, LLC, a global entity aimed at empowering men and women to change the world.

Dr. Reid is also a seasoned international trainer, ministry life coach, motivational speaker, solution strategist, and bestselling author. He serves as the executive director and CEO of BARN Community Housing, and has also developed a series of empowerment workshops, coaching techniques, and conferences aimed at helping individuals stay focused in solution mode.

Learn more at
www.your1solutioncoach.com

Suited for Success

George Rice III, a native of Toledo, Ohio, is an award-winning educator, coach, speaker, and the chief empowerment officer and founder of The Rebound 4 Success Institute based in Washington, D.C. Coach Rice earned his bachelor's degree in psychology and master's degree in mental health counseling from Morehouse College and Bowling Green State University respectively.

With over 15 years of experience in teaching, coaching, consulting and mentoring, Coach Rice has impacted the lives of countless students, athletes, coaches, and professionals by helping them transition from learners to leaders to champions. In 2013, his article, "Who is Joe Black?" was featured in *Sheen Magazine*.

To connect, email him at
info@coachrice.net

About the Authors

Larry Scott Blackmon is the vice president of FreshDirect Public Affairs. He earned a B.A. in communications and black studies from the State University of New York College at New Paltz, and a master's degree in public administration from the Metropolitan College of New York. Larry is also a graduate of the John F. Kennedy School's Executive Leadership program at Harvard University, an alumnus of the Coro Leadership New York program, a member of the Pi Alpha Alpha National Honor Society, and president of the Harlem Chapter of Alpha Phi Alpha Fraternity Incorporated.

Having nearly 20 years of public service, community development, and government experience, Larry has worked with numerous federal and state representatives. He has been recognized as #14 in "The 50 Most Powerful Community Leaders in the Bronx" and was named one of the "40 under 40" people to watch by *The Network Journal* and other publications.

Dwayne Booker was born and raised in Brooklyn, New York, and received his education through the public-school system. He completed high school at the prestigious Brooklyn Technical (Tech) High School and received his bachelor of arts from CUNY, York College.

Booker currently resides in Maryland but continues to call New York his home.

About the Authors

Chaplain Derrick J. Redmond is a native New Yorker, a devoted husband to his lovely wife of 23 years, and a dedicated father to their four amazing children and beautiful granddaughter. Derrick's dedication to serving his family, community, and peers has led him on a journey in providing pastoral care. He has worked as an educator for 20 years, and is the dean of students at Cultural Arts Academy Charter School where he facilitated them into receiving the prestigious and global Lighthouse School status.

A sought-after mentor, motivational speaker, private security facilitator, entrepreneur with ForSmiles Inc., and NYSTF Chaplain, he was one of the first honorary members of the International Christian Brotherhood (founded by his pastor, Rev. Dr. A. R. Bernard, to train men in Christ-likeness as a standard for manhood). He is also the director of the boy's mentorship group, Manproof. Chaplain Derrick's mantra is, "Success is our protection."

Paul Coty is an advocate, a national inspirational speaker, and a champion for children and families across the five boroughs of New York City. As vice president at Young Life NYC, Paul exemplifies modern transformational leadership and innovation in urban ministry. With relentless drive and a commitment to helping young people find their higher purpose, Paul currently spearheads the most dramatic expansion of Young Life's global youth ministry in the world's largest and most challenging market—New York City.

Today, Paul is an ordained pastor and expert advisor in the fields of multicultural and urban youth ministry, and visioning/strategic planning. For almost two decades, Paul's professional career has been focused on serving Christ, developing strong leaders, and ministering to the needs of kids. Paul presently lives in Long Island, N.Y. with his wife, Shauniqua, and three children, Paul, Jeremiah, and Savannah.

About the Authors

Steven Carter serves as the Senior Pastor of the Mount Ararat Church in Brooklyn, N.Y., and the founder of Steven Carter Ministries. He is the adopted and only child of Eugene and Mary Carter. A graduate of Thomas Jefferson High School in Brooklyn, N.Y., Carter earned his bachelor of arts degree in religion from Morehouse College, and a master of divinity degree from Duke University.

Carter has become a sought-after preacher, motivational speaker, lecturer, and panelist. In 2014, he served as the Keynote Speaker for a White House event on behalf of the United States Administration for Children and Families.

A proud member of Alpha Phi Alpha Fraternity Incorporated, Carter is also the author of the critically-acclaimed book, *Resurrection from Rejection: Healing from 7 Areas of Rejection in Your Life*, and has been featured in *Ebony Magazine*, *CNN iReport*, *Ambition Magazine*, and numerous others.

Learn more at
www.steven-carter.com

Craig Palma is a leading employment strategist, certified federal career counselor, and federal job search trainer who has helped hundreds of people obtain employment with his weekly and monthly seminars for schools and nonprofit organizations. Craig's unique employment strategy's and step-by-step employment process teaches people how to obtain employment in this tough economy. He is tireless when it comes to helping people navigate the difficult process of obtaining employment with the federal government.

Craig has worked for such Fortune 500 companies as: Verizon, AT&T, Sprint, Errand Solutions, the East New York Youth Alliance, the Police Athletic League, Junior Achievement, Macy's, FEGS, STRIVE, and Goodwill of Greater New York. Recognized throughout Corporate America and the nonprofit community for his charismatic, dynamic, and uniquely engaging presentations, Craig is a powerful motivational speaker and employment trainer whose *10 Step Employment Pocket Guide* has empowered others to overcome adversity and obtain employment.

About the Authors

Xavier Porter, MPA is a seasoned mental health counselor and community relations expert with over 20 years of experience as a leader in the areas of strategic planning and facilitation, public affairs, advocacy, crisis management, community and government relations, and business etiquette. He possesses a well-rounded set of experiences in the nonprofit, government, university, and health care industries. A firm believer in rights for all and breaking the stigma of mental illness, Xavier continues to work for a large behavioral health agency, providing integrated services to an array of disabled individuals.

Among his areas of expertise are: Brand, Social Media, and Content Strategy; Digital Marketing; Budgeting; Analytics and Insights; Strategic Branding; Radio; Print; Media Corresponding; Photojournalism; Editing; and Public Relations.

Born and raised in Jamaica, N.Y., Xavier currently resides in Harlem. He is a single father raising his 14-year-old daughter who is his pride and joy.

To connect, email him at
xporter456@gmail.com

Suited for Success

Troy Harrison, a native of Brooklyn, New York, has been a New Jersey resident for over 25 years. In 1991, Troy opened the first professional natural hair salon in New Jersey— Afrakuts House of Nu, creating a business that embodied the seven principles of Kwanzaa. As a sought-after natural hair care consultant and educator, Troy continues his involvement and leadership in positions such as: educator and platform artist for the World Natural Hair and Beauty Show and Bronner Brothers International Hair Show, founding member of the Natural Hair Care Association and the Black Men's Forum, and member of the City of Orange Planning Board.

A servant of his community, Troy is a captain in the City of Newark Fire Department, where he recruits and trains firefighters. In his spare time, Troy mentors community youth in hopes of inspiring them to find success through roads less traveled.

About the Authors

David Marquis grew up in South Bronx, New York, where he found sanctuary at the Boys & Girls Club, propelling him to earn an athletic scholarship for basketball to West Texas State University. After college, David enlisted in the U.S. Army and trained as a corp engineer.

Upon his return from the Army, he worked in the entertainment industry for 20 years, leading to his current passion in entrepreneurship: cologne. In November 2013, David launched his first cologne, RISE, followed by his second scent in June 2016, POISE de Parfum.

Norman Grayson is a savvy health advocate, entrepreneur, and ambassador of change who is on a lifelong mission to help people pave the path to longevity. His top priority is to create a legacy that will continue empowering others for generations.

Throughout his multifaceted career, Norman has received multiple awards and certificates from various esteemed ministries and entertainment groups. He currently serves as a founding member of a thriving health and fitness company. He has also been involved with numerous ventures including: international radio interviews, speaking engagements, and health fairs.

Beyond the realm of wellness, Norman enjoys dancing, going to amusement parks, quiet time, and attending church. Norman is happily married and the proud father of three beautiful children. Above all, he cherishes nothing more than spending quality time with his wonderful family who inspires him to be his very best.

About the Authors

Sherrod Kersey, born and raised in New York City, grew up amongst diversity and therefore developed an eclectic mentality. As a youth, Sherrod had an innate gift that allowed him to draw, design, create, or arrange anything in a unique way. After teaching himself to sew, he is now a self-taught clothing designer who creates customized clothing.

Today, Sherrod designs all types of clothing including: caps, t-shirts, sweatshirts, sweatpants, jeans, shirts, hoodies, jackets, sneakers, and boots. Sherrod has incorporated his creations into his brand, TRENDITY.

Learn more at
www.trendityclothing.com

Darrell J. Edmonds is an innovator, community servant, and thought leader. He is the founder of the nonprofit organization, Friday Is Tie Day, Inc., so called because it encourages young men to wear ties to school on Fridays. The mission of the organization is to build men through male youth mentoring and responsible fatherhood.

Since its genesis in 2013, the group has grown from seven teens at one high school to over 75 teens at 12 high schools. They meet monthly for lessons on goal-setting, college awareness, and leadership development.

Darrell is happily married to Janine Edmonds who is a guidance counselor at Oakcrest High School. They are the proud parents of Olivia (13 years old), Keilani (7 years old) and Jessica (1 year old).

About the Authors

Dimitri David Jr. is pastor and founder of Grace Fellowship, a division of Dunamis Christian Center International. Dunamis Christian Center International was founded in the year 2000 as a humble Bible study in Pastor David's home. As the congregation grew, DCCI relocated several times to accommodate growth. In obedience to the will of God, the growing congregation held its first Sunday service on the July 1, 2001, and launched the ministry of Grace Fellowship in September 2014.

As a teacher and expositor of God's Word, Pastor David is an able agent to lead the charge in communicating the Word with boldness and simplicity. In addition to leading a successful ministry, Pastor David is a motivational speaker and compassionate counselor. A public servant for over 15 years, Pastor David's ultimate desire is to inspire, motivate, and encourage those he teaches.

Cyriac St. Vil was born and raised in Brooklyn, New York, to parents that emigrated from Haiti in the mid-60s. One of six children, Cyriac grew up under family values that emphasized education, faith, and love for your fellow man. After excelling in elementary and middle school, Cyriac received a Regents diploma from one of the top specialized high schools, Brooklyn Tech. He then went on to major in business administration at Kingsborough Community College before leaving to begin his venture as a business owner.

With the spirit of an entrepreneur, Cyriac opened his first business at 24 years old. In addition to running a small business, Cyriac also coordinates the educational program "Learning Through Nature" which is currently being taught in three learning institutions within New York City. Cyriac is also a founding member and spokesperson of the nonprofit organization, 500 Men Making a Difference.

About the Authors

Conrad W. Higgins is the founder and CEO of Higgins Realty Group, LLC, located in Brooklyn N.Y. He specializes in residential and commercial sales, leasing and property management, and he offers real estate consultation services to home owners, nonprofits, and businesses.

Conrad holds an associate degree in biology from Kingsborough Community College and a business degree from NYACK College. He has been licensed with the New York Department of State as an agent and a broker for over 16 years. Conrad's goal is to take his business to the top of the real estate industry, becoming a conduit to launch other businesses and help the community.

Conrad is also an elder and leader in his local church. He has been married for 18 years and is the father of two wonderful boys. He has a passion for cartoon drawing, studies ancient history and their civilizations, and admires great architecture.

Ty Brown, "The Band Man," is a youth advocate, entrepreneur, and renowned community leader. He is the founder of Brooklyn United Music and Arts Program, which impacts over 500 students annually. Additionally, Ty is the CEO of Big Deal Fundraising, Big Deal Prints, Big Deal Trophies, and United Transportation.

While living life with purpose, Ty currently has consultant contracts with the Universoul Circus, The Brooklyn Nets, and 1199. He has been featured in *Black Enterprise*, the *New York Times*, and was "New Yorker of the Week" twice. He is the former Band Director at Monroe College and works very closely with HBCUs across the nation to provide scholarship opportunities to young people from Brooklyn.

Ty has created many brands of amazing competitions for youth to share their talents. He has also established an office in South Africa to assist young people within the country he now calls home.

CREATING DISTINCTIVE BOOKS WITH INTENTIONAL RESULTS

We're a collaborative group of creative masterminds with a mission to produce high-quality books to position you for monumental success in the marketplace.

Our professional team of writers, editors, designers, and marketing strategists work closely together to ensure that every detail of your book is a clear representation of the message in your writing.

Want to know more?
Write to us at info@publishyourgift.com
or call (888) 949-6228

Discover great books, exclusive offers, and more at
www.PublishYourGift.com

Connect with us on social media

@publishyourgift

www.ingramcontent.com/pod-product-compliance
Lightning Source LLC
Chambersburg PA
CBHW071559080526
44588CB00010B/952